History and Genealogy of the Kings of Dahomey

Tome 1:

Kings, Queens and Amazons of Dahomey

Based on African Local Oral History and Accounts by Western Visitors and African Historians

Dallys-Tom Medali

Translated from French by the Author

Solara Editions

History and Genealogy of the Kings of Dahomey - Tome 1
Kings, Queens and Amazons of Dahomey

Translated from the French Original by the Author himself

© Copyright 2020 - All rights reserved
DALLYS-TOM MEDALI

ISBN 978-1-947838-38-3

Solara Editions
New York, Cotonou, Paris

Cover Design: Dallys-Tom Medali
Translation: Dallys-Tom Medali

Pages web: www.livres.us / www.heroafricain.com
Emails: editeur@livres.us / dallys@livres.us
Facebook: @ArtLit7 / Twitter: @AfroBooks

Contents Overview

Tome 1: Kings, Queens and Amazons of Danxomè (**This Book**)
- Acknowledgements
- Genesis
- How names work in the Fon culture
- New discoveries and revelations
- The patriarchs
- Details on the kings and queens
- Panegyrics of the kings and queens
- Contributions of the amazons women warriors
- Origins of some cults, voodoos and towns names
- Lists of Monarchs of various kingdoms in Dahomey
- Lists related to European presence in Benin
- Lists related to Benin's political history
- List of photos and illustrations
- Bibliography
- Other Books by the same Author
- Other Books in "The House of Dallys" Series
- Contacts

Tome 2: Genealogy Files of Princess Aligbonon (**Other Book**)
- Acknowledgements
- Genesis
- How names work in the Fon culture
- The Parents of Princess Aligbonon
- The Descendants of Princess Aligbonon
- The Direct Connections
- 114 family trees
- Index of dates
- Index of places
- Index of individuals and names
- List of photos and illustrations
- Bibliography
- Other Books by the same Author
- Other Books in "The House of Dallys" Series
- Contacts

Contacts

If you have any information, archives, documents, or suggestions to share with us, or if you want to order more copies,

Please reach out by mail to:

PO-BOX 04-0143, Cotonou, Republic of Benin
or
5829 N 29th St Omaha, NE 68111, USA
or
email: dallys@livres.us

Acknowledgements

I am deeply grateful:

To the Lord

who gives me life and strength,

To my kids Andrew and Athéna, and their mom Mireille

for their support,

To my parents Ida, David and grandma Marguerite

for their teachings

To my deceased parents A. Medali, A. Tokpo, E. Segle Houegbadja., and all their ancestors,

for the inspiration and the roots,

To you who bought this book

and/or contributed to its improvement.

―z-z-z-z-z-z-z-z-z―

Genesis

This series of twelve books is the result of a life of research and tells the story of many lives.

I seriously started working on it back in 2009 after leaving the Danish company MAERSK in Cotonou. The project continued slowly and steadily, before ramping up in 2017 after my departure from the global accounting firm BDO in New York. This became my primary full-time occupation between 2017 and 2019 for the original version, and into 2020 for the translation.

We owe it to our forefathers and our children to leave as complete and detailed possible, a picture of our roots and origins. If we don't work on our history and our genealogy, who will do it for us? The task is daunting and never-ending, but we can be proud of the significance and the importance of our contribution.

This specific volume (Tome 1 of Book 10 of the Series) covers the history of the Kings of Danxomè, a major African kingdom in what is currently the country of Benin, formerly known as Dahomey, a name that it inherited from the aforementioned kingdom.

Tome 2 which has already been translated in English and published, is all about the genealogy of the kings and queens and is a little more boring (like any genealogy book), though just as important as this volume.

I always admired the Kings of Danxomè and constantly learned as much as possible about them from an early age. But I never intended to dedicate a specific book of my own to them. However, when I was mapping the numerous trees of my large set of families, they became a component so important of the bigger puzzle of my ancestral lineage, that it became a moral duty to share some of the amazing information I gathered and all the knowledge I fact-checked about them, with both the general public and the scientific community. A significant portion of these facts, events, and stories have never previously been written or published.

Most people stay away from history books because they are often voluminous, dusty and are packaged in what can only be called an academic writing style. Authors seem to entangle themselves in various discourses about their literary sources rather than presenting their best understanding of the facts and events in a simple and clear prose that the reasonable reader can digest or even enjoy. I decided not to fall in that trap here. I will include sources when they are available, pertinent and add to the understanding of the stories. For some of the sections that came out primarily of oral tradition and/or conversations and testimonies by people either still alive or already deceased, there will be no reference to cite in a traditional sense. This work can be the source in which future researchers, writers, history buffs, Africa lovers and Benin patriots can dig to carry on the mission.

Migrations by the Fon, Ewe and Kwa People

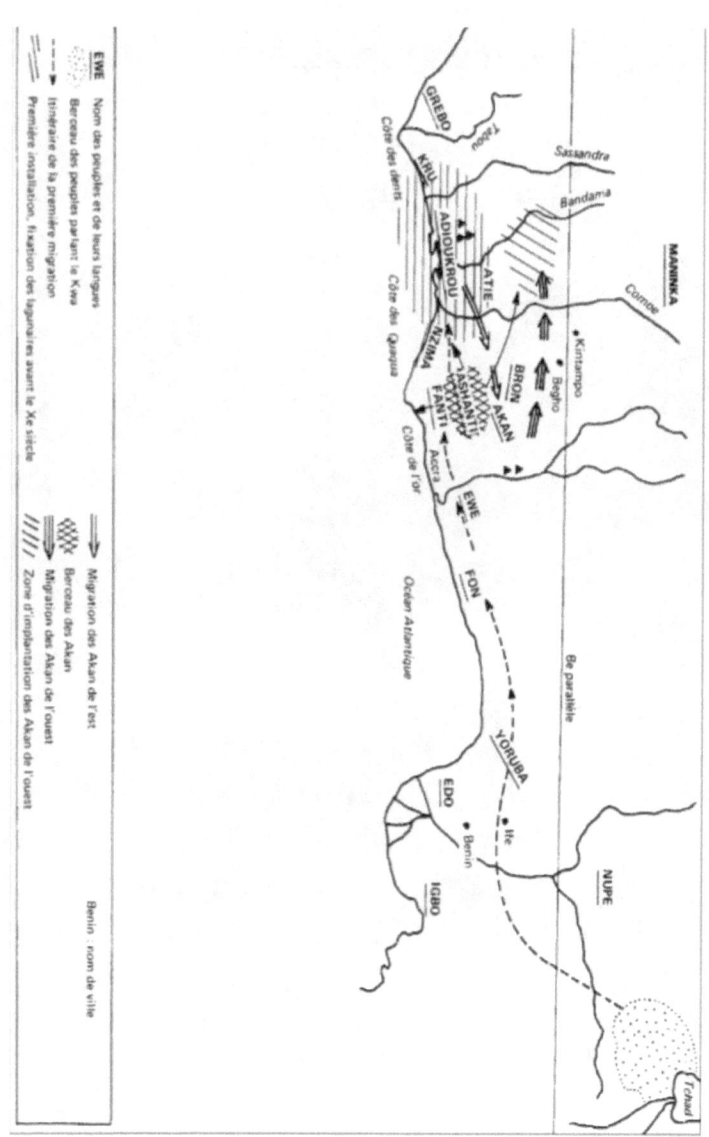

Map of Dahomey in 1892

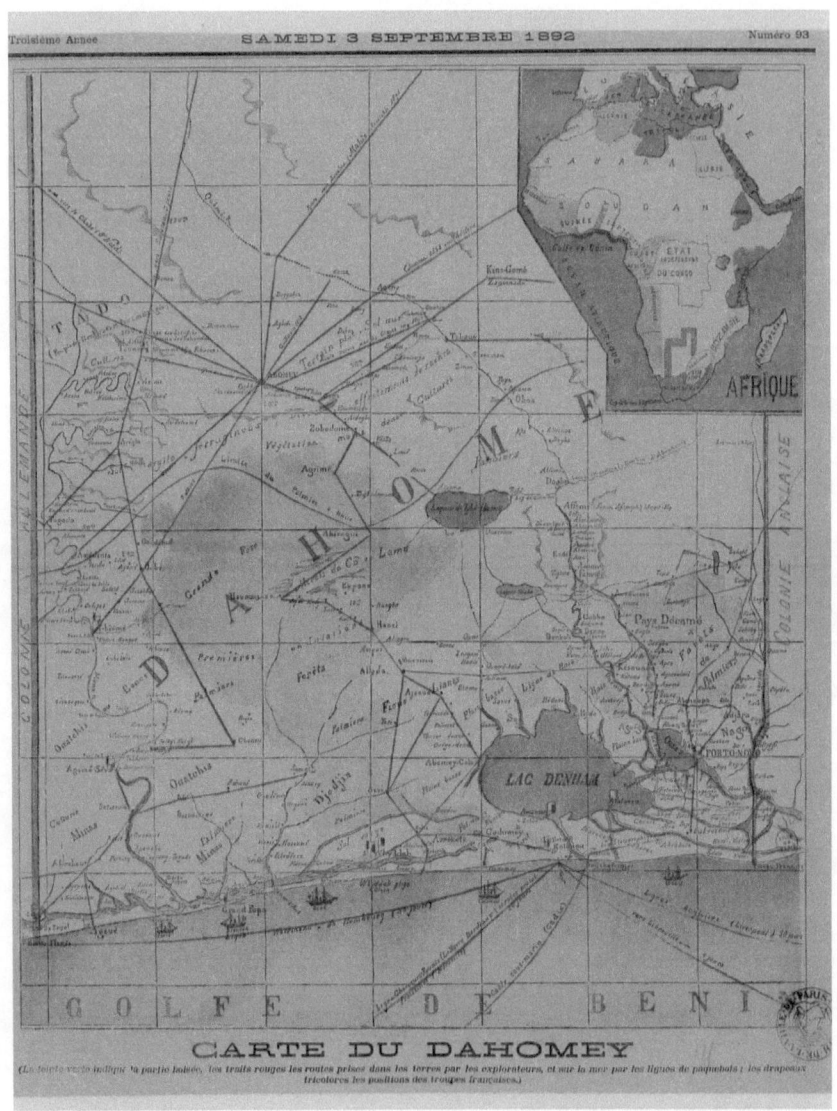

Current Map of Southern Benin

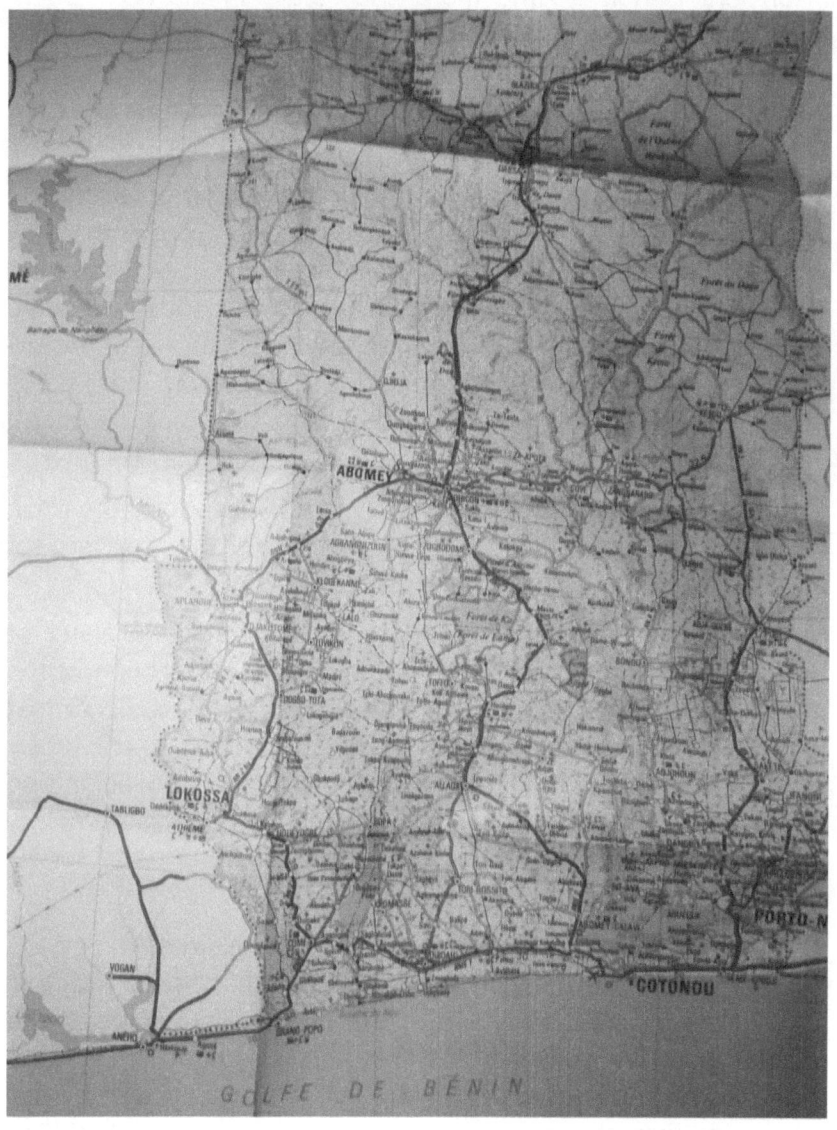

How names work in the Fon culture

In ancient Dahomey, and more specifically in the Fon, Goun, Mahi, and Adja traditions, Names were given, taken and used quite differently from what came to be during the days of the colonial administration and became common practice after the country's official independence from France in 1960.

Your Name was not your birthright or something given to you once and for all when you were born, and for you to carry all your life. It was instead a succession of badges of honor and awards that you would obtain following some deeds or events. Those accomplishments could be heroic, infamous or simply routine. Sometimes, the Name could come from something beyond the control of the individual and to which he didn't contribute.

Children did receive a first name at birth; based on the year, season, month, day, time of the actual birth or the "baptism" of the child or his presentation to the community.

Sometimes the Oracle would choose the first name either at birth or long before birth. That name will be a reflection of the special destiny predicted for this newborn or will indicate that the child is the full or partial reincarnation of a previously defunct ancestor of the family. Sometimes the child wouldn't be a reincarnation of that ancestor but would only be his protégé, meaning that the ancestor is a personal guide and protector for the newborn.

The child can also be named based on how his mom's delivery occurred. Was it a complicated birth? Was he/she born before term? Was the child a twin? Did the other twin(s) survive? Did the mom survive? Did the child first show his head or his hand or his leg? Did the child come with all his body parts and in full health, or was the child disabled or handicapped? Was the pregnancy a daunting and long experience for the mother? Twins always get special names and correlated names. The order of birth can also inform the name (first child, in-between, last child). The gender plays a part too. Did the previous children from other pregnancies survive up to this one?

Generally speaking, the traditional civil registry in Danxomè had the following components:

1. The predictions of the Fa oracle before the birth
2. The predictions of the Fa oracle after the birth
3. The baptism and/or presentation of the newborn to the moon, to the community and/or to the ancestors
4. The scarification rituals (houegbigbo and/or atindjidja)
5. The circumcision rituals (adagbigbo)
6. The initiation of the teen or young adult to a profession, trade or labor
7. The initiation to various religious practices, cults or voodoos
8. The initiation to various secret societies
9. The engagement to a future spouse and the dowry
10. The wedding
11. The celebration of heroic acts and remarkable achievements
12. Other important events
13. The pre-burial rituals
14. The burial rituals
15. The post-burial rituals
16. The annual or cyclical customs and celebrations in honor of the ancestors and the deceased of the family or community.

The order of occurence of those events is flexible and some happen simultaneously or never happen at all.

When the European invaders came, the last name became very important and useful to differentiate and separate people belonging to different families, casts and ethnicities. That brought a lot of confusion and mistakes. First, family names were long sentences and often hard to pronounce if you are not fluent in the specific native language. Those names were then shortened, twisted, mangled and distorted. Children of a same parent will find themselves with different names or different spellings of a same name.

Sometimes two people living in different eras or in the exact same time period and geographic location have the same names or very similar names. It becomes challenging to distinguish which events relate to one person and not the other. Polygamy and out-of-marriage births were also very common, and divorces were rarely formalized.

All these explanations are important to explain some situations you may encounter when going through the genealogy and historic events. Someone who is unaware of those nuances can easily get lost. The reader is invited to keep an open mind.

Abridged Genealogy of the Kings, Dallys-Tom Medali

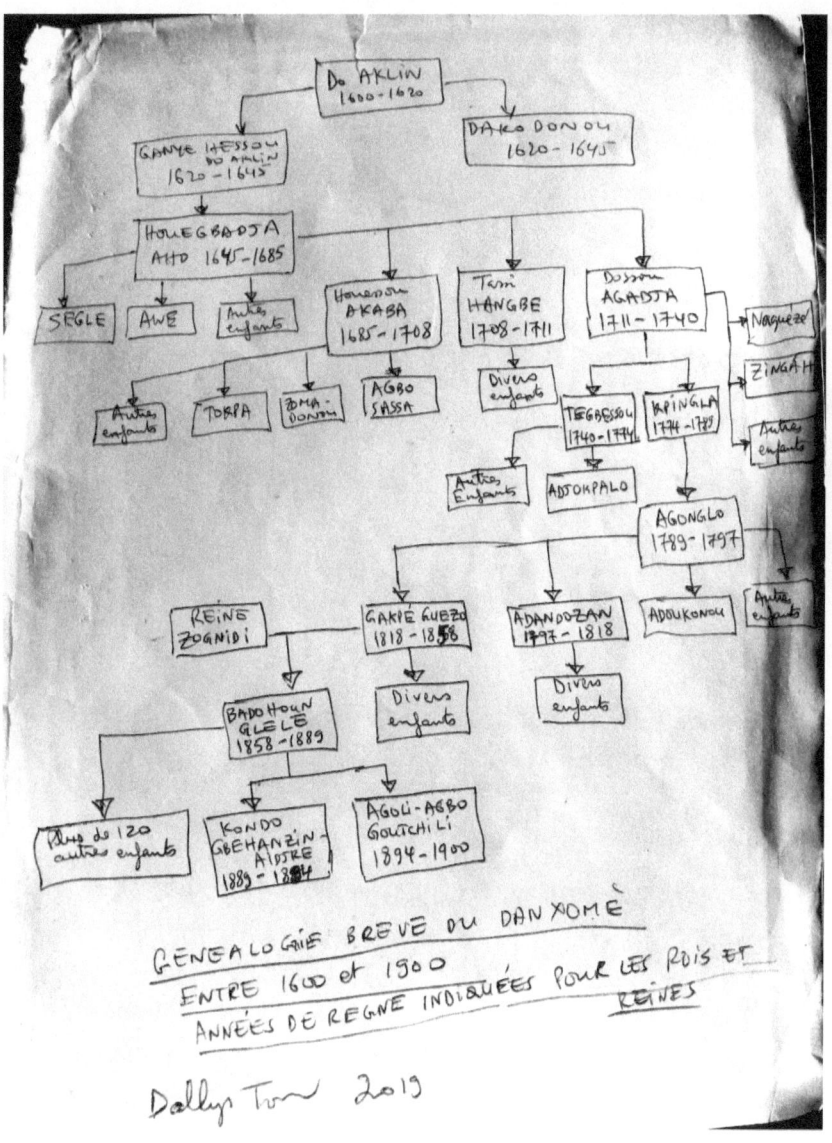

Tome 1:
The Kings of Danxomè

Royal Symbols in Danxomè

AFOKPA (started with King Houegbadja) - Royal Shoes - They give legitimacy to the newly anointed King.

AVOTITA - Woven and decorative cloth used by the King.

AWE - Umbrella - A mark of prestige that also protects against the burning African sun.

KATAKLE - Tripod stool on which the King sits.

MANKPO - royal scepter, (récade in French)

SO (gun) and **HWI** (sword) - Most of the Kings and Queens were experienced warriors and former generals who personally lead the army in battle.

AHOSU-ZINKPO - Royal throne

Chronology of the Kings of Danxomè (1600-1900)

X - Various Patriarchs through 1600 in Tado and Allada

1 - Chief Do Aklin (1600 - 1620)

2 - King (the usurper) Dako Donou (1620-1645)

3 - Honorary King Gangnihessou (1620-1645)

4 - King Aho Houegbadja (the founder) (1645-1685)

5 - King Houessou Akaba (1685-1708)

6 - Queen Tassi Hangbé (1708-1711)

7 - King Dossou Agadja (the conqueror) (1711-1740)

8 - King Bossa Ahadé Tegbessou (1740-1774)

9 - King Kpengla (1774-1789)

10 - King Agonglo (1789-1797)

11 - King Adandozan Madogugu (1797-1818)

12 - King Ghézo (the great) (1818-1858)

13- King Glèlè Kinikini (1858-1889)

14 - King Kondo Gbèhanzin (the warrior) (1889-1894)

15 - King Agoli Agbo (1894-1940)

X - Various Honorary Kings (1940-present)

This chronology is likely different from what you are accustomed to or what you previously saw online, in books or on canvases and engravings. Perhaps Queen Tassi Hangbé was nowhere to be seen on that old common chronology. Perhaps the years of King Adandozan were left in blank. There was perhaps no differentiation between Do Aklin (the father) and his son Gangnihessou Do Aklin.

When foreign writers compiled our history, they made some mistakes and alterations that carried on and sometimes influenced later our own understanding. The mistakes were often due to linguistic barriers and to insufficient or unavailable information.

Take the meaning of the name of King Behanzin for instance (Gbè hin azin bo ayi djrè). In primary school in Benin, children are taught an erroneous French explanation that translates to "the world holds an egg desired by the earth". But "Djrè" is not to be confused with "Djro" and has nothing to do with desire.

If you visit King Behanzin's palace in Djimè (Abomey, Bénin), you will see a metallic panel on which the artists, advised by the elders, properly captured the meaning of his name. The panel reads "le germe de toute manifestation de la terre" which can translate to "the germ of all manifestations of the earth".

Your elementary teacher probably told you that "Kondo" means "le requin" in French or "shark" in English, when in fact the word in Fon for "shark" is "Gbowhele".

To learn about the real meaning of the names of King Behanzin, please refer to his section later in this book.

Fon is a complex language that puts a lot of emphasis on vocal tones and inflexions. One word can have more than four different pronunciations, each with its own meaning. Sometimes you can even have multiple words with the exact same spelling and the exact same pronunciation. The classical example is the sentence "yon nou". It is a tough ask to expect foreign writers to master all those nuances.

Archeologic research such as the one conducted in Agongointo (Bohicon, Benin) improve our understanding of the past. The same thing happens when private or official archives and collections are digitized and shared with the public. That's how we are able to learn a lot of details about the wars between Dahomey and France from the standpoint of the French military observer.

Sometimes, a breakthrough can come from an old traditional song placed in its proper context. But the best insights often emerge at the feet of the old and wise relatives. Important things that were once destroyed in accidental or criminal fires can thus come back to life.

We will cover all those elements whenever we feel that they can enlighten and enrich the reader without muddying the main storylines.

THE PATRIARCHS

The patriarchs are not counted among the Kings of Danxomè, but they should be highlighted because they are the ancestors of those Kings and Queens. Some of them also ruled back in Tado or in Allada.

The main ones are:
- King TOGBE ANUI (TOGBUI-ANYI)
- Prince AGASSOU KOKPON
- King ADJAHOUTO LANSUHOUTO LANDE
- King KOKPON DOGBAGRI
- Chief DO AKLIN

TOGBUI ANYI (TOGBE ANUI, TOGBE ANYI)

TADO was the capital-city of the old kingdom and the Adja Civilisation. It was founded circa 1000 AD and its golden age was between XVth and XVIIth century AD. It is regarded as the cradle of the Adja, Fon, Ewé, Ayizo, Xwla, Xweda, Guin, Goun, Sahwe, and many more ethnicities. Although we now know that before TADO, they migrated from the current territory of Nigeria, and aeons before that, from the common birthplace of the entire human race in East Africa.

TADO was once called "EZAME" with "EZA" being a tree name. Thus "EZAME" means "In the Eza woods". Back in those days, the tribes were often afflicted by diseases and many children would die. Drought and hunger were common occurence. That was until the arrival of the legendary TOGBUI-ANYI, who offered to heal everyone if they agreed to make him King. He succeeded and was crowned. His first official act was changing the town/kingdom name to "Tado" which means "to jump over".

From that day on, all the bad luck, troubles, diseases will jump over and avoid the kingdom. A feast is held every year in August, up to this day to commemorate that salvation. The celebration is called "TOGBUI-ANYI". Although the official kingdom is no longer what it once was, it is currently ruled by its 187th King whose power is mostly ceremonial and symbolic.

AGASSOU KOKPON

Not to be mistaken with KOKPON DOGBAGRI who ruled over Allada many centuries later and whom we discuss later in this book.

King ADJA AHOSSOUHO of Tado had many children. One of them was a gorgeous princess called ALIGBONON. One day while she was bathing with her servants, a spirit or a young man took the physical appearance of a panther and approached the group. The servants ran for their life but the princess was not afraid and didn't flinch. We will never know for sure if it was really a panther or if "KPO" (the word for "panther" in Fon) was just the name or the nickname of a strong handsome young man. All we know is that KPO seduced the princess and she became pregnant and later gave birth to a baby that grew up to become a brave youg man named AGASSOU.

AGASSOU had many children and grandchildren. He is the ancestor of all the AGASSOUVI, ALLADANOU, and most of the Fon People, Goun People and many other ethnic groups of Southern Benin. "AGASSOU" means "the husband from above". "Above" refers both to the sky and to the spiritual world. ALIGBONON certainly chose that name to honor the memory of the mysterious being that made love to her on the banks of the river and that she never saw again.

ADJAHOUTO LANSUHOUTO LANDE

One of the sons of AGASSOU was called LANDE and would later be known as LANSUHUTO because he was a great hunter of wild beasts and big games.

LANSUHUTO decided one day to become king in Tado but was rejected by the elders because he was not at the top of the royal succession hierarchy. LANDE murdered ADJA , a prince who was the next direct in-line for the throne.

"ADJA" was both the name of the people, a geographic designation and a title used by Kings and princes in the ancient kingdom. So the fact that the legend simply names the killed prince as "ADJA" doesn't give us enough information about his full identity. Anyway, from that day on, LANDE was to be known as ADJAHOUTO (the slayer of Prince ADJA).

A few versions state that LANSUHUTO is ADJAHOUTO's son, but that is unlikely.

The murder triggered a full-blown battle. Thus LANDE, his brothers, sisters and all the descendants of AGASSOU had to run away from the kingdom to save theirs lives. They first went to the town of SAHOUE, before continuing to reach a group of AYIZO villages that will later become ALLADA. Adjahouto is therefore the founder of the Allada kingdom. In his honor all the following kings carry the title of "Adjahoutonon". The exact year of that migration is unknown. Some European historians claimed that Allada (Ardres, Ardra) was already known in the western world around 1200. The chronology of Allada kings currently available to us goes back to 1400.

The Ayizo people (Adja-yi-zo, meaning Adja people who went far away) themselves came from the Adja kingdom decades earlier. They were already present on the Allada territory and had their own organization and chiefs before the new wave of migrants came.

I chose the years 1400 as the most plausible timing in my analysis based on all avaiable evidence.

Adjahouto died in 1440.

KOKPON DOGBAGRI

Not to be confused with AGASSOU KOKPON his ancestor who lived and died aeons earlier in TADO.

KOKPON DOGBAGRI was a remarkable King of Allada who ruled for two decades from 1590 to 1610. The end of his rule led to a schism and the birth of the kingdoms of Abomey and Porto-Novo. Three of his children went on to be kings in three different kingdoms.

MEDJI followed in his father's steps and ruled over Allada.

DO AKLIN lead a migration towards to the Zou region and ruled there from 1600 to about 1620 before dying and passing the baton to his sons GANYE HESSOU and DAKO DONOU.

ZOZERIGBE lead the migration towards the Oueme region and contributed to the future creation of the HOGBONOU kingdom (future Porto-Novo) where his son TE AGBANLIN ruled between 1688 and 1729.

Brief genealogy diagram

Tome 2 of this book goes in depth with the genealogy of the kingdom starting with Princess ALIGBONON. But a short overview of the TADONOU ALLADANOU AGASSOUVI lineage can be provided here.

TOGBE ANYI Founder of TADO
|
(...) Various TADO Kings
|
King **ADJA AHOSUHO** of TADO
|
Princess **ALIGBONON** + KPO the mythical panther
|
AGASSOU KOKPON
|
LANDE LANSUHOUTO **ADJAHOUTO**, Founder and King of Allada (1400-1440)
|
King ADJA AHOLUHO of Allada (1440-1445)
|
King DE NOUFION (1445-1458)
| |
King DASSOU (1458-1470)   King DASSA (1470-1475)

(continued)

King DASSA (1470-1475) d'Allada
|
King ADJAKPA (1475-1490)
| \
King YESSOU   King AZOTON (1495-1498)
(1490-1495) & (1498-1510)
|
AKOUDE, AMAMOU, AGAGNON, AGBANGBA, HOUEZE
(1510-1520) (1520-1530) (1530-1540) (1540-1550)
(1550-1560)

                                              |
— — — — — — — — — — — — — — — —AGBANDE (1560-1580)
| | | |
KINHA   MEDJI1   AKOLI   **KOKPON DOGBAGRI**
(1580-1585) (1585-1587) (1587-1590)   (1590-1610)
                      / | |
                  MEDJI2 **DO-AKLIN** *ZOZERIGBE*
                  (Allada)   (Zou)   *(Oueme)*
                    /   ∧ |
            LAMADJE **GANYE/DAKO** *TE-AGBANLIN*
                / | |
           Other   **HOUEGBADJA**   *Other Kings*
        Kings of Allada (1645-1685) *of Porto Novo*
                          |
                Other Kings of Danxomè

The order of succession of the Kings of Allada is accurate. However I was unable to totally certify whether a king is the son rather than the brother of the previous king.

Details about the Kings of Danxomè

It is now time to cover the royals of Danxomè, specifically:

- The twelve canonical Kings commonly listed on decorative cloth artworks sold in Abomey.
- Chief Do Aklin, who can equally fall under the patriarchs or kings umbrellas. I opted to count him among the Kings but with the title of "Chief".
- Queen Hangbé,
- King Adandozan, and
- King Agoli Agbo.

Chief DO AKLIN (1600 - 1620)

DO AKLIN was the leader of the migrants who came from Allada to settle on the Zou plateau (Houawé, Abomey and neighboring cities and towns). It was not his father KOKPON DOGBAGRI (as some historians have posited) because he stayed in Allada where he ruled from 1590 to his death in 1610.

That migration occurred at the end of the sixteenth century. 1600 is a commonly agreed year used to mark that event in the historic timeline.

DO AKLIN did not use the title of "King" because he still revered Allada as the real kingdom. He was an influent chief, like other local chiefs in this new area. The newcomers needed to first get rid of the local chiefs ruling over the Guedevis people before they could consolidate their power and establish the kingdom of Danxomè.

DO AKLIN gave birth to many children but only Gangnihessou and Dakodonou were famous and influential. Many elements from DO AKLIN's rule mix-up with his son Gangnihessou's rule because unlike his brother Dakodonou, Gangnihessou the eldest, adopted his father's name after he passed away.

King GANGNIHESSOU Do Aklin (1620-1645)

Emblem: bird, drum and a spear

Motto: I am the biggest bird and the loudest drum. Nobody can prevent the bird from singing and the drum from sounding.

Ganye Hessou was also known under his father's name "Do Aklin". He was the eldest and legitimate heir to the throne.

Panegyric of Gangnihessou in Fongbe and in English

Gànixêsu aobobo

Gangnihessou, be applauded

Xësu ao yaya

The male bird everyone cheer and applaud

Ajo ma no yi Dàxomê

Thieves are unwelcome in the Danxomè

Gànixêsu kpakpà do akoto

Gangnihessou isn't afraid to visit his family

Akpadi ma no no nênu

You cannot cook krinkrin (corchorus olitorius) soup with akpadi

Adi za

The potash is not enough

Nênu zä

The krinkrin soup is not enough

Akiza gbatö

The conqueror of Akiza village

Akiza'xòsu Akpakpo hutò

The slayer of Akpakpo, king of Akiza

B'agala dele

Example of courage

Ganixêsu lo adètò

Gangnihessou the brave

Gangnihessou was the eldest son and Vidaho of Do Aklin and was destined to be the next chief/king of the AGASSOUVI people after his dad died. Being still attached and respectful to the customs and rules of Allada, he decided that there was no better place to go to have himself formally appointed as the next ruler.

Taking advantage of his brother's departure, Dakodonou who was shrewder and stronger physically, immediately auto-appointed himself as the next king and sat on the throne in Houawé.

When he got back from Allada, Gangnihessou was very surprised and upset by the new order. Being of the gentler and conciliatory kind, and unwilling to create a schism or a fratricide war in the fairly young kingdom, Gangnihessou exiled himself to the town of Cana with some of his loyal relatives, friends and servants except for Houegbadja his older son that he left in Houawé as a sign of good faith and no ill will. Houegbadja stayed in Houawé with his uncle Dakodonou (Dako) for many years before migrating somewhere else.

Dako was able to consolidate his authority and power on the territories under his control, by eliminating a couple of GUEDEVI chiefs. However two of the biggest chiefs were still evading his yoke: ADINGNI and DAN. ADINGNI was ruling over all of current day Bohicon including Houawé (where Dako was making a name for himself) and Cana (where Gangnihessou went to exile himsef). DAN was ruling over current day Abomey and all the surrounding towns and villages. It would take a couple of decades before Prince Akaba succeeded in killing DAN during the rule of his father Houegbadja. That's why many historians give credit to Houegbadja for that achievement.

Young Prince Aho (future Houegbadja) deserves however full credit for neutralizing ADINGNI. He used ruse to achieve his goal and thereafter beheaded ADINGNI, and brought the head as an unexpected gift to his uncle Dako.

In those days, in the Fon/Adja culture, whoever vanquished the ruling king or chief, was rewarded for his bravery with the crown and became the next king. But Aho Houegbadja who just defeated and killed King Adingni, was still a teenager and his uncle had no intent to bow to him or let him rule over him. So Dako congratulated his nephew and suggested that he pick some soldiers and servants and install a new settlement somewhere else to be their king as he proved deserving to be. Dako suggested he could go to the lands near current day Abomey. It was a tainted gift because as previously stated, there was another king/chief ruling over those lands : the ruthless chief Dan.

Aho, who was fearless, agreed to his uncle's offer and launched an expedition to settle near current day Abomey. At first the relationship with the new landlord was peaceful because Aho in his wisdom came bearing gifts and asking for permission before starting his settlement. Chief Dan himself granted them the first plots of lands.

On those lands, Aho built a big palace-like house and protected it with fortifications and a large trench. That was the birth of Agbome (Abomey). The news of the novel imposing and beautiful architecture quickly spread and gave birth to a lot of resentments and some plots to kill Aho. Those threats were coming simultaneously from chief Dan and from Aho's own uncle whose kingdom in Houawé was starting to falter after the best fighter left town.

Dako sent words to his nephew Aho, stating that he was giving him the option of returning to Houawé so they could team up once again. Aho refused firmly and in the process took on a new name as "Houegbadja". Aho was in essence asking why would a freed fish deliberately offer to return to the net in which he was once caught. His uncle was the net and Aho was the shrewd fish who successfully freed himself.

Aho Houegbadja then proceeded to invite his own father Gangnihessou who was starting to get bored in Cana, to come join him in Abomey where exciting new things were happening. Gangnihessou quickly agreed and rejoined his son. There was a rule according to which Fon and Adja people were prohibited from making themselves King whenever the individual's own father was still alive and present. By respect, Aho Houegbadja symbolically let his father be anointed and seated as the honorific King. But in reality he was already busy crafting and executing his vision for what was to become one of the most significant kingdoms of the African continent.

In appearance and during customs and feasts, Gangnihessou was King and would remain until his death which likely occurred in 1645 when Houegbadja officially became the monarch. The exact date is unknown.

The Exodus of the AGASSOUVI people and the origin of some villages names and deities names

Origin of the AGASSOU deity and the DOMELOKOE deity

In early times, all the ALLADANOU people worshiped the AGASSOU deity or vodoun and were known as the AGASSOUVI people. The AGASSOU deity was a representation of the divinisation AGASSOU who was a forefather and patriarch of all the ALLADANOU people. AGASSOU who lived long before the exodus from TADO was an ancestor for all those people.

The priests who took care of the AGASSOU deity were known as AGASSOUNON. My maternal grandmother Marguerite descend from the AGASSOUNON family tree. My paternal grandmother Elisabeth SEGLE HOUEGBADJA was at some point a major priestess of that deity and managed a convent in Abomey.

Shortly after the departure from Allada, a dispute started and split the migrants in two opposed camps:

1- The camp of the true genetic descendants of AGASSOU including Chief/King DO AKLIN and his sons and daughters, the princes and princesses led by GANGNIHESSOU and DAKO and all their servants.

2- The camp of friends and allies who also believed and worshipped AGASSOU. That side was led by DANGBALI and his three brothers GBOGBO-HONNOUMATON, DJOKOUNDAHO, and AFOYO along with their families and servants.

One day, some elements from the first side forbid people from the second side from worshipping AGASSOU, claiming that since he was not their ancestor he couldn't really be their god. The leader of the second side in a feat of anger, pointed his finger to a nearby iroko tree ("LOKO" in Fongbe and "chlorofora excelsa" for the scientific name) that was standing in a valley ("DOME"), and replied: <<Since you are forbidding us from worshipping AGASSOU, we will from now on start worshipping this iroko tree in the valley.>> Thus was born the DOMELOLOKOE deity which was a sacred iroko tree. The priestly duties were assigned to DANGBALI and his descendants.

Origin of the towns of HOUEGBO and AKOUTA

In spite of the new religious divergence, the migrants continued their journey together. Their next camping ground was the town of DAWESSA known for an abundance of bamboo trees.

Here, princes, princesses, friends and servants all gathered and decided to make peace and to resolve their religious disagreement. After reaching an understanding, they decided to give the area a new name and called it "HOUEGBO" which means "reconciliation" in Fongbe. This was to serve forever as a reminder that they were able to reconcile and stay united. They also created a new shrine to the AGASSOU deity in the village of DAWESSA in the town of HOUEGBO. That village is still known today as HOUEGBO-DAWESSA.

The migrants continued their journey until they reached HOUAWE where they decided to resettle. Here they brought their traditions, knowlege and cults.

DANGBALI built a big shrine for the DOMELOKOE deity. Later he went to the city of Abomey and created a massive palm-tree farm near the village of GNIDJAZOUN. He was appointed as a chief over a big landmass that went from the frontiers of

SEHOUN and DOKON all the way to the banks of the Couffo river, including the town of TANGADJI (where the KEDJE people lived.) DANGBALI left his brother AFOYO in charge of the farm. AFOYO had two sons: AKPOLI and DOUBOGAN.

DANGBALI left GNIDJAZOUN with his remaining two brothers: GBOGBO-HOUNNOUMANTON (whom he stationed in the town of ADADALI) and DJOKOUNDAHO (whom he stationed in the town of DOVOME).

To thank DANGBALI for all his devotion and expansion work and to keep that area united, the King (either HOUEGBADJA or his dad or his uncle), asked for the creation of a new vodoun to be known as the AKOUTA deity and that a shrine be built in its honor. That deity gave its name to a new town.

The noble DANGBALI was survived by one son named AVOKANLIN. More information will be provided on those patriarchs and families in a future book by this author on the ANATOHON family history.

King DAKO DONOU (1620-1645)

Emblem: a sledgehammer and a jug of indigo

Motto: Dako killed Donou as easily as he broke and rolled the indigo jug. ("Dako hou Donou bô zin bligbo")

One day as he was going around in the bushes, Dako stumbled upon his nemesis Donou who was a chief among the Ayizo people. Donou was busy preparing a mixture of indigo dye in a big terra-cotta jug and didn't notice the presence of Dako. Dako jumped on Donou and killed him. He then cut his body to small pieces, put them in the jug and started playfully rolling it around town. Some people claim that this incident popularized the indigo dye through the Danxomè kingdom. Even to this day, people still use woven fiber mats (nattes), clothes and baskets, died with the indigo color.

Panegyric of Dako Donou in Fongbe and in English

Donu ni axòsu bo meto no ci akpo
Donou, you who became King by making another one fail

Daködonu ni axòsu bo mêto nò ci akpo
Donou, you who became King by making another one fail

Donu gâ xwi bò me ku
Donou sharpens his sword and the man dies

Bulukutu hutò
He who killed Bulukutu (one of the indigenous chiefs of the Zou region)

Asino wiwe hutò
He who killed the stepmother who was too nosy

B'agala dele
Example of courage

Dakòdonu lo adetò
Dakòdonu the intrepid

Brother of Gangnihessou, Dako took power in the latter's absence. Gangnihessou went momentarily to Allada to perform the enthronement ceremonies. This story is already told in the previous section (under King Gangnihessou).

The year of Dakodonou's death and end of reign is not known for sure. Some historians use 1645 which is the year in which Houegbadja began his reign. But this year is rather the year of death and the end of the symbolic reign of Gangnihessou, father of Houegbadja. It is possible that Dako Donou also died the same year as his brother or a little before (most likely scenario) or a little later. It is also possible that Houegbadja out of respect, waited for the death of his father and his uncle before his coronation. What is certain is that the seat of Dakodonou's power was in a different location (Houawe) from that of Gangnihessou and Houegbadja (Abomey). After the death of Dakodonou, Abomey became the indivisible and undisputed capital of the kingdom of Danxomè.

Dakodonou did not have any biological heirs, either because erectile issues (according to what my grandfather explained to my father), or because he was infertile, or due to a retaliation from the gods.

Several families, however, consider themselves descendants of Dakodonou (and with good cause). During his reign, Dakodonou adopted a multitude of children whom he raised as his own. Moreover the offspring of an individual's slaves were also considered the offspring of the individual himself and carried his name in those ancient times. It was even forbidden to discriminate or to declare that such is a real child and that such is not a legitimate child.

King Aho HOUEGBADJA, the Great (1645-1685)

Sassa-ho-gueli (elephant hunter)

Emblem: fish and trap net

Motto: The fish that escaped the trap does not return to it.

"houé gb'adja, man yi adja"

the fish that came out of the trap is not ready to return. This is an allusion to the pitfalls set up by his uncle Dakodonou for his refusal to stay by his side in Houawé.

Panegyric of Houegbadja in Fongbe and in English

Dada Aho de ma na kpo

King Aho will defeat his ennemies.

Sasa nò xala ko

The hornbill bird has the laughter of the hyena (The hornbill bird is one of the legendary animals of Dahomey. It is credited with many virtues, including that of scaring off predators as fierce as the hyena.)

Do gba agli gwì nu

Your troops broke down the walls.

Kpiso ma no hu sunu

It is not by shaking him that one kills a strong man.

E va do to bo no kuzu to

He covered the country and imposed his tribute on it.

To galagala vi Lësu

Courageous son of this country

Su nu hwe le di lele kpe to

Just like the moon, the sun spreads everywhere (Poetic pun on "hwe" which means both "sun" and "fish" in fongbe)

Mè të gbe ma të sè

You can pull up most grass, but not quackgrass

E të dada Axo kaka se kpô e na ko alòmènu wè me

Just like quackgrass, nobody can pull up King Aho

Gle huzò bò xwä mià sa

Farm labor was so hard that the woman sold her land.

E kpôn kaka bo do e sa è

That woman also deserved to be sold. (The woman had promised the King to clear a whole field by herself, counting on the help of her lovers. But after the defection of the help she expected, she had to sell herself with her field to avoid death.)

Dada hutò

He who killed Dada (Name of a local chief from whom that official title of the Kings of Abomey was subsequently derived "DADA".)

Ajotï kpodo Lugwïkpà hutò

He who killed Ajotï and Lugwï (two Nago chiefs)

B'agala dele

Example of courage

Dada Axo kaka lo adëto

Aho, intrepid King forever

Houegbadja (Houégbè adja) is the real builder and founder of the capital of Danxomè: Abomey, which will later be called "the city of the sons of HOUEGBADJA". He built his palace in the middle of fortifications and ramparts, "agbo min" that the French simplified in the form of "Agbome" then "Abomey". The palace is protected on one side by the forest. His successors will build their official palaces in the extension of that of Houegbadja.

Houegbadja codified and promulgated the constitution (Danxomè Ka-soudo) and all the rules governing the functioning of the kingdom. Houegbadja made laws with the obligation to respect them on pain of death. Recognized by the people as "King", he appointed ministers, the most important of whom was Mehu.

Houegbadja won against the Guédévis. He extended his kingdom by subduing the hostile chiefs and also the Adja, like their King Tokpli who came to rescue certain villages and stop the expansion of Abomey. The region of Oungbégamé, submitted as well as those of Agouna and Djalloukou (populated by Yoruba / Nago). Ahossou Soha Gbaguidi left the region and went to settle with his family at the foot of the hills in Savalou to avoid trouble.

Houégbadja went to Cana (Kanan) in the temple of Agassou to be recognized by the ancestors and to learn about the great secrets of the kingdom. After this ceremony, the country belongs to him as if he had bought it. He assigned a role to each minister, and instituted the ceremonies which would later be called the great customs. Every year or sometimes every two years to prove to the ancestors the loyalty of the King who continues to follow in the path they have mapped out, and to prove to the people that the ancestors agree with the actions of the present ruler. Another ceremony instituted by Houégbadja is the "houéwou lilè" or "annual bath." When the first yams are harvested, it is a purification ceremony that takes place in a river towards Zogbodomè.

With his official wife Nanye Adonon, Houégbadja had two twins (the twins being highly revered in Danxomè): a boy called Houessou (who will become King Akaba) and a girl Tassi Hangbé (who will also become queen briefly after Akaba). He also had other children including a boy who would be called Dossou Agadja and was a powerful and conquering King.

Houegbadja's influence on Danxomè is immense because it begins during the reign of his uncle Dako and his father Gangnihessou, continues under his own reign and continues at least during the reigns of his three direct children Akaba, Hangbé and Agadja. This period starts from 1620 to 1740 at least, that is to say twelve decades. That's why it is fair to consider him as the most influential ruler of the kingdom.

Origin of the villages of GNIDJAZOUN and DOKON

AWESSOU, long before he was even called that, was chief and overseeing a large territory which included the current location of the city of GNIDJAZOUN during the rule of king HOUEGBADJA. Thieves regularly stole from his cattle of oxen and slaughtered them for meat to eat. When AWESSOU was taken to the scene of the crime, he exclaimed: "ZOUNGBO E MIN YE NON DJA YIN TCHE LE DE O DIE" which became

"GNIDJAZOUN". It means: "This is the bush where my oxen are often slaughtered."

He also added: "NAN GBO LEDJE DOKON DE" which later became DOKON. It means, "I'm going to have to move around here (to keep an eye on my cattle)." AWESSOU was now known as the chief of DOKON.

Princess AWE and her DOKON lover

King HOUEGBADJA had very beautiful daughters. They were very pretty. One of them called herself AWE. She deeply loved a young independent prince, chief of DOKON. History did not reveal the initial name of this young chief who also honestly loved AWE. Mutual open love led the them to marriage. From then on, he was known as AWESSOU, that is to say the husband of princess AWE.

This AWESSOU is the ancestor of NANWOUI AWESSOU who is the mother of my paternal grandmother Elisabeth SEGLE HOUEGBADJA (HOGBONOUTO AWANSIKINDE).

AWESSOU organized his court and had many servants. In the afternoons everyday, a man called KPALIN held a golden gong and sung the praises and exploits of AWESSOU.

The love adventures of princess HANGBE and GBOGBO HOUNNOUMANTON: the origin of the name ALLADAYE

The handsomeness of the elegant GBOGBO-HOUNNOUMANTON grabbed the fragile heart of the charming princess HANGBE, daughter of HOUEGBADJA, and she suddenly fell in love. GBOGBO-HOUNNOUMANTON also could not resist the dazzling charm of the great princess. The two attracted each other but came up against the class barrier. The princess was of the upper royal class. GBOGBO-HOUNNOUMANTON although an artist of great renown, was not of princely rank. But he dexterously played and danced the TOBA rhythm, and the populace adored him. He was very skillful and gallant, but he also initiated to the occult sciences. This last skill will be very useful to him when his future wife HANGBE becomes Queen of Danxomè after the death of her twin brother, King AKABA. His fame earned him the nickname of GONON ALLADAYE. In its complete form: GO DJE HON NON HIN ALLADAYE which means: the gourd attacked by the guinea worm, keeps the shadow of ALLADA.

Children of King HOUEGBADJA

- SEGLE (his first son)
- King HOUESSOU AKABA
- QUEEN TASSI HANGBE
- King DOSSOU AGADJA
- AWE (whose husband became AWESSOU)
- NAN DEDAGBE
- Other children

King Houessou AKABA (1685-1708)

Emblem: warthog (or boar), saber, chameleon
Motto: When the warthog looks up to the sky, it gets slit.
Slowly, gently, the chameleon reaches the top of the kapok tree.
dè dè kaba kaba aganman no lia hun

Panegyric of Akaba in Fongbe and in English

Xwesu fiägodo

True son of this house (also one of the symbolic names of Akaba)

Yeûmè

He who is more than the others

Akwè yeûmè

Rich in cowries

Je yeûmë

Rich in pearls

Avo yeûmë

Rich in loincloths

Je yeûmè

Rich in pearls

(the King is the Jëxosu, King of pearls, the only one to hold the wealth)

Nugbigba azö dokpo, azö dokpo mö nò di yeûmè

It is not what you exhibit at once that shows your wealth.

Yaxëze kpolu hutò

The one who killed Yaxeze (Yahasse) while he was crouching (Yahasse is an anthropophagous monster-man (or a cannibal leader of the Ouemenous according to some versions), whom a valiant servant of Akaba defeated during a battle at Lissezoun)

Tägbe gbatò

He who conquered the village of Tangbë

(Village located around Allada, conquered at the same time as those of Sinhoué, Gboli, etc.)

Tägbe'xòsu Ayiza hutò

He who killed Ayizâ, chief of the village of Tangbé

Gboli-Akata gbatò

He who destroyed Gboli-Akata

(This village was near Allada. After destroying it, King Akaba took away all the inhabitants to found a new village of the same name not far from Abomey.)

Aglwi hutò

He who killed Aglwi (Local chief of the region of Allada who had allied with Galinu Pala, King Adja of Tokpli, to overthrow the young dynasty of Abomey)

B'agaia dele

Example of courage

Xwesu Akaba lo adètò

Akaba, intrepid son of this house.

The mysterious cannibal YAHASSE

Under the reign of King AKABA, a cannibalistic monster-man decimated the population from the west of the kingdom to the center. They called him YAHASSE. He took men and women, and crushed their skulls greedily. A general panic spread through the kingdom and necessitated a vigorous and decisive counterattack. King AKABA designated HOUEMEHO and assigned him the mission of bringing back the head of YAHASSE.

At first glance, the reader might think that YAHASSE KPOLI was an irrational primitive monster. In fact, other accounts provide more precision and let us know that he was a bit like the security head and war chief of the Guédévis under the reign of chiefs like AWESSOU and DAN. Someone's hero is someone else's monster. He is one of the reasons why the ALLADANOU could not simply annihilate and quickly dominate those who lived before them in the region. It was only after his death that AKABA could definitively establish the grip of the ALLADANOU people on the region.

The powerful hunter HOUEMEHO, once at home, hastily got ready. He placed all his powerful talismans around his neck, arms and hip, dressed and put on his shoes. He then took his weapons and plunged into the bush. He walked several days and nights westward without ever meeting the monster. HOUEMEHO went a little further north through the rainforest and after a few days of walking, turned east and headed straight.

Suddenly he stopped in his tracks: the monster man was in front of him. YAHASSE had just got up from behind a tree, shook his bulky head, sniffed the air, and began to run. HOUEMEHO chased him through forests and savannas, and arrived at LISSEZOUN. YAHASSE out of breath, stopped and faced HOUEMEHO who shot him. The monster man fell over with his hands on his knees and died but did not fall. HOUEMEHO jostled him for a long time but did not succeed in making him fall. The information was brought to King AKABA who came to the scene. He also tried to knock him down, but couldn't. The King asked himself: "what position to adopt in order not to go to death?". YAHASSE's head was cut off and transported to AKABA's palace where it was kept in a safe place called <DJIHO>. This head with miraculous virtues allegedly contributed to the rout of some enemies of Danxomè and gave the kingdom many victories.

Chief Dan, who had approved the installation of the ALLADANOU TADONOU people, had become very annoyed by their incessant requests for further expansion of their territory, especially since they were already very close to the houses of the GUÉDÉVI people. He then asked with sarcasm if Akaba (who was still Prince Houessou at the moment), wanted to install his new houses in his belly. Akaba ended up taking him at his word and built the new constructions "in his belly". Danxomè = In the (me) belly (xo) of the chief Dan (Dan).

The Gédévis and the Alladanous had until then lived in a coexistence based on a mixture of tolerance and mistrust. One day Dan tried to kill Akaba by having a trap dug on his usual route: a ditch whose entrance was camouflaged. Akaba was walking that day with his dogs going in front of him. As the dogs fell and perished in the ditch, Akaba understood that he was dealing with an ambush and that he had barely escaped death. Akaba confronted and killed Dan the formidable leader of the Guédévis in a duel. Afterwards, he placed the first stake (like the first stone) of the new palace of Danxomè on the remains of his deceased opponent.

The name "Danxomè" which will become "Dahomey" with the French deformation therefore started with King Akaba, while the name "Agbomin" which would become "Abomey" came from his father King Houegbadja.

Houessou Akaba ascended the throne at the advanced age of 50 years. This may be why he took as a symbol the chameleon which slowly but surely reaches the top of the kapok tree.

He wears his father Houégbadja's own royal sandals and creates thereby this tradition which makes sandals an important emblem of royalty. Akaba continued the installation of the Danxomè institutions, in accordance with the instructions of his father Houegbadja. He instituted the role of prime minister which he entrusted to his friend Hâssou now called Migan.

The Yorubas and the Ouéménous attacked the city of Abomey by surprise, then were pushed back. The chiefs of Sinhoué, Sahé and Gboli on the left banks of the Couffo are defeated and submit to the King of Danxomè. Akaba's troops, already active on multitude fronts, failed against the Guins at Kindji.

The Europeans landed in Ouidah and Djekin, bringing smallpox with them as they did in the Americas. So very early on, the disease began to spread among populations not yet immunized. Akaba also succumbed to it while still fighting against the Yorubas and the Ouemenous.

Agbo Sassa, son of Akaba, being too young to govern, especially when the kingdom was at war, the twin sister of the deceased King (Tassi Hangbé) ensured the regency after a decision of the Grand Council. This was very displeasing to the prince Agbo Sassa and to the future king Dossou Agadja.

AKABA's children

- AGBO SASSA
- TOKPA
- ZOMADONOU (ZOMADOU)
- Other children

Queen Tassi HANGBÉ (1708-1711)

Emblem: warthog or wild boar (like Akaba's emblem)

Motto: When the warthog looks up to the sky, it gets slaughtered (like Akaba's motto).

She has the same Emblem as her twin brother and predecessor Akaba.

AKABA had already contracted the smallpox infection which would later be fatal. It was in the midst of a military campaign by his army against Yoruba / Nago territories. Still lucid but bedridden, he invited his twin sister HANGBE and offered her to dress like him and lead the troops and continue the campaign. HANGBE complied with his brother's decision and valiantly fulfilled the mission. It is this subterfuge proposed by AKABA himself which will influence later the council in charge of choosing the next ruler.

Smallpox which is a highly infectious and easily noticeable disease would have been a distraction for the troops, just like the whispers about the future of the kingdom without its ruler. This is why even the news of the King's death was not quickly published. Smallpox was brought in by western traders who landed in the port of Ouidah. The people of Danxome at first, did not know how to avoid it or how to cure it.

The night of King AKABA fell on the kingdom of Danxome - that is to say that the King died. His only heir AGBO SASSA was still very young. This situation was favorable to his uncle AGADJA who secretly coveted the throne. The royal council decided otherwise. Indeed, Princess HANGBE was appointed Queen responsible for ensuring current affairs until AGBO SASSA becomes of age. The royal cannon was fired with roaring thunders. Everyone bowed to the court's decision. AGADJA looked for a way to overturn this great decision. He would succeed a few years later. A crown prince had to show intelligence, cunning and wisdom and then demonstrate his courage, his firmness, his tenacity, his bravery and his great power. Prince AGBO SASSA did not yet have the qualities to be Head of a great kingdom like ABOMEY. He still had a lot to learn and should be patient.

Hangbé was the almost identical twin sister in terms of physiognomy of King Houessou Akaba. She reigned under the cover of her deceased brother, and disguised like this one to prevent the enemies of the kingdom from taking advantage of a period of mourning or transition.

Hangbé ruled as a regent in place of AGBO SASSA, legitimate heir of AKABA while keeping the attributes of his twin brother AKABA. She was supported and assisted by her husband ALLADAYE until the latter's death.

Hangbé also gave the hand of his sister Nan Dédagbé (daughter of Houegbadja) to her husband ALLADAYE so that she could keep him company during her absences for wars.

Nothing can be hidden indefinitely. HANGBE's reign had long been overlooked. The fact that her ascencion to the throne itself was not highly publicized (lest enemy kingdoms profit from it) was also a contributing factor. Thus, Western travelers and historians often overlooked it out of ignorance. The official artists of the kingdom of Danxomè do not mention her on their paintings and loincloths. It was not until mentalities and customs evolved for a few centuries that her memory was rediscovered and is being progressively restored. The Kings, princes and priests of Danxomè, however never forgot her: whenever it is time to honor the royal spirits, she is always included in the proceedings and receives her share of sacrifices and libations.

The queen had five children with her only husband: three boys, a girl and a still-born baby called MEDEWONNOU (a pregnancy that she put in the crack of a wall before going to war. According to the legend, upon her return, she retook the pregnancy from the wall to give birth the same day. Obviously the child did not survive that ordeal and was buried next to the wall. The grave is marked by a stone in the HANGBE palace up to this day. For a rational mind, this could have just been an abortion story mythologized.)

Children of Queen Hangbé

AGONHON

ANAGONOU TOSSA

HOUESSOUGBE

SEBOGLON

MEDEWONNOU (the still-born)

The Army of Danxomè (Illustration, 1793)

The famous Danxomè customs festivities, (Illustration, 1793, Archibald Dalzel)

King Dossou AGADJA Trudo, (1711-1740)

Emblem: caravel (warship)

Motto: Atin dja agadja man gnon zo do. (No one can set a large felled tree with all its branches on fire; it must be cut down first.)

The caravel or boat on his emblem represents the capture of Savi and Ouidah with a crux symbolizing the Christian religion that the missionaries introduced to the kingdom during his rule.

The ascension of AGADJA to the throne

AGADJA who coveted the throne remembered that Queen HANGBE had a man in her life. Logically, the queen's husband or lover became de facto king. The idea that GBOGBO-HOUNNOUMATON (ALLADAYE) could become King or exercise the function under the cover of his wife Queen HANGBE did not sit well with the royal family. One night, AGADJA ambushed GBOGBO-HOUNNOUMATON in front of the queen's portal, captured and killed him. His grave was hermetically sealed. It was then that AGADJA took the nickname DOSSOU. The news spread quickly, reached the ears of Queen HANGBE who became heartbroken and immediately relinquished power. At daybreak, the royal the cannon was fired. AGADJA seized power, ascending the throne under the name of DOSSOU-AGADJA. It was in 1711. King DOSSOU-AGADJA (YAN MAN DJO HOXO LO BO GNI DOSSOU that is to say: the man not being born after twins but who nevertheless called himself "the closer of hole"). Dossou was the name given to the male child born to a family that previously birthed twins. Agadja was not the next brother to be born after the twins Akaba and Hangbe, and as such is not a real "Dossou" but he took the name anyway.

The new king summoned his nephew, the young prince AGBOSSASSA in his palace and initially informed him that the decision of the court was still applicable and reassured him as for the future return of the power in his hands once he becomes adult.

AGBOSSASSA and the porridge bowls

A few years later, the legitimate heir AGBOSSASSA appeared one morning at the palace of King DOSSOU-AGADJA in order to assert his rights. He felt he was now mature enough to become a ruler. He was warmly welcomed and installed together with his followers. They were served water and then liquor (sodabi) according to local customs at that time.

Shortly afterwards King DOSSOU-AGADJA came and sat down and ordered that the first bowl of porridge be presented to the young prince. The latter dipped his tongue in it, found that it was without sugar or honey, so he put the bowl back and didn't finish it. The second bowl was handed to him. He brought it to his mouth and noticed that it was a bowl of very sweet porridge. As such he drained the content of the bowl all at once.

King DOSSOU-AGADJA explained the riddle to him: "Thus, in Abomey, royal power is comparable to this bowl of sweet porridge. Once we taste it, we no longer put it back. We do not put it back until we are dead. >>

AGBOSSASSA angrily left the palace with his followers and went home. He picked up all his belongings, gathered his faithful companions and then gave instructions on the new destination of the group. His caravan crossed the ADJAHI market and was followed by other faithful who came to the market. They set course for the North, arrived at THIO and then moved to ASSANTE. From that day, Prince AGBOSSASSA rejected the panygeric and the identity of the AGASSOUVI people (the royal family) and adopted those of the AHANTOUNVI people.

Later war expeditions launched against the North captured some descendants of AGBOSSASSA who were brought back to ABOMEY and resettled in DOGUEME on a domain called <<AYIMINTONDJI>> (literal translation: "On our domain").

Agadja was born in Abomey in 1673 and died in 1740. His face marked with scars from smallpox, he was of medium height and stout, intelligent and slender. Agadja was so brave and remarkable that he was nicknamed "Trudo" by the English. His exploits were known around the globe.

Impatient and tired to wait for his eventual turn, and not wanting to take the risk that little Agbossassa would grow up and ascend the throne, Agadja devised a coup d'état to overthrow his sister Hangbé: He first decreed that he was "Dossou", that is to say the child who comes after the twins Akaba and Hangbé. Which was not correct since he did not follow them immediately. This is why the Fons say "Agadanou Dossou", that is to say an artificial "Dossou" of the last hour.

Agbo Sassa went into exile and went to settle with his family in Mahi territory in Ouessé.

Panegyric of Agadja in Fongbe and in English

Cakucaba agidi wolo
Cakucaba, the very powerful charm

(Cakucaba is a magical name of Agadja)

Agidi wolo
Very powerful charm (talisman)

Lo wuli nu tô ma do adikà
When the crocodile catches something, the river does not put it on trial. (reference to how Agadja stole the throne from his older sister Hangbé and his nephew Agbossassa)

Xla fâ b'avù bò
When the wolf moans, the dogs hide.

De kaka de do to
Bien qu'étant nombreux, ils doivent se taire
Although there are many, they must be silent.

Ku hu nu ma u xölö
No one can take revenge on death itself.

Savinu Hufô hutò

He who killed Huffon king of Savi

Anagonu Savi hutò

He who killed the Nago and Hxedas people living in Savi

B'agaia dele

Example of courage

Dosu ho-yi-tò lo adetò

The intrepid Dossou who seizes the boats of the Europeans on the sea.

Conquering Allada

The kingdom of Allada was enriched by trade with the coastal kingdoms which traded with the Europeans and the slave raids which were sometimes directed against the Fon people. Agadja who wanted to stop the raids and wished to cut his dependence on Allada for the acquisition of weapons (he wanted to trade directly with the Europeans), began to plot an offensive.

There was a big ceremony in Allada to which king Agadja was invited along with King Houffon of Savi. Houffon praised his wealth and made fun of Agadja, who instead of being offended decided to be cunning and to punish the culprit at a later time.

In March 1724, Agadja and his troops invaded and decimated the kingdom of Allada. The violent campaign which lasted only three days left thousands of deaths and eight thousand prisoners, a good part of which would later be sold as slaves to the Americas especially the island of Hispaniola or St-Domingue or Haiti. The future parents of the legendary Haitian general Toussaint Louverture were among those slaves.

Conquering Savi and Ouidah

Agadja had heard of the wealth of the coastal city of Ouidah. The travelers tell of the wonderful things that the European traders import from fabulous and distant countries (Yovotomé) and exchange for slaves. Ouidah is therefore the door that Agadja must conquer.

In 1724 Agadja asked king Houffon for permission to trade freely with the Europeans. Houffon had at that time two cannons and a lot of guns which he bought with 85 slaves. He refused to let Agadja trade directly because he knew that if Agadja came to Ouidah, he would quickly lose control of his territory. He probably already heard what happened to the kingdom of Allada.

Agadja tries to march on Sahé and seven times his army is paralyzed and driven back by the thunder of guns and cannons they had never seen before.

Houffon offers Agadja a deal of one rifle for each slave; but being clever, he has the weapons altered so that they cannot be immediately used against him and his people. Agadja, knowing nothing about weapons, was happy that he finally acquired the terrible new weapons.

After some time, the Danxome soldiers got used to the thunder of the new weapons and no longer ran away. However, they didn't yet know how to use them properly. The guns Houffon sold Agadja were tampered with and missed some parts. It took two men to operate them. One man would hold the weapon and another one would fire it.

Thinking that he already had what it took, Agadja attacked Houffon's army once more, but was beaten again. Houffon pursued him as far as Ouégbo-Ahouétanou.

Seeing the gravity of the situation and facing the risk of losing his previous conquests, and having finally understood that he was deceived with defective weapons, Agadja considered it prudent to delay the war. He came up with a clever plan. To spy on Houffon and to buy some time, Agadja gave him one of his daughters, princess Na-Guézé as wife, as a sign of goodwill and a gesture of peace between the two kingdoms. The princess went to settle in Savi with all her followers and a lot of presents.

Houffon and his powerful army, emboldened by the many times they defeated Agadja, continued to catch and sell the Fon people of Abomey as slaves. They also committed many crimes as they pleased with no fear of repercussion. Around the same time, the Popo allied with the Houédas against Agadja, thinking that he was finished and that he would be unable to resist a final assault on Abomey itself. But Agadja had other tricks in the bag.

In 1727 the army of Agadja set a camp around Savi at a place that would later be called Savi Na-Guézé. They managed to identify the gun powders depot of the kingdom of Savi and to dump water on all the stock. Thanks to Amazons disguised as simple servants of Queen Na-Guézé and who succeed to enter the city discreetly without being detected by the guards, the mission was a clean success. Afterwards, Agadja and his troops easily defeated the kingdom of Savi and its capital Ouidah; as well as a multitude of other nearby kingdoms and territories.

It was under the reign of Agadja that the Danxomè kingdom developed a true navy for the first time, with a multitude of ships stationed in Ouidah on the coast. They took advantage of the expert swimmers, fighters and fishers of the coastal territories that were now under the control of Abomey. The Atlantic coast and the other territories beyond Ouidah will be definitively occupied and permanently administered in 1741 under the reign of king Tegbessou.

Campaigns against the MAHI people

Agadja undertook three military campaigns against the Mahi of Gbowélê and Paouignan, to acquire slaves to be exchanged for weapons. The Mahis resisted and started harassing the Danxomenous. Furious, Agadja executed several of their leaders previously captured as prisoners of war, before later managing to defeat them.

The capture of Djekin / Koutonnou / Cotonou

The incursions of Agadja started impeding the normal order of business and the traffic of slaves on the coast. At the behest of the Dutch traders who provide them with plenty of weapons, the inhabitants of Djêquin rebel and prepare to resist against the army of Abomey.

In March 1732 the kingdom of Djêquin (Djékin), previously a vassal territory of Allada, on the southern coast of Godomey, is defeated and submits itself to king Agadja. The city is captured and certain Europeans traders who were arming, assisting, or even fighting alongside the people of Djekin, are arrested.

The wars against Oyo

The reign of Agadja, the conqueror is filled with incessant wars to enlarge the kingdom and expand trade and exchanges with the Europeans. Unfortunately, Agadja had less success on the eastern front and had to bow his head in front of the Yorubas of Oyo.

Alafin and his powerful army of Oyo Ojidji, composed of intrepid horse riders, attacked the Danxomè with the support of the Fon people of Agonli. They forced Agadja and his troops to take refuge on the banks of the Mono river.

With the fall of Savi and Ouidah, and feeling the Danxome threat approaching their own doors, the Houéda chiefs asked for help from the Alafin of Oyo and the Yoruba army. The Ayonous (Yoruba) agreed and came to sack Abomey. The Yoruba invasion could also have been an autonomous and opportunistic enterprise not influenced by the appeal of the Houedas and Popos.

Rather than losing his entire army, Agadja preferred to withdraw beyond the Mono River, leaving his capital under the control of the Yoruba. The Mono river subsequently flooded and served as a defensive barrier.

Tradition reports that during the war council, the Gaou (general-in-chief or army minister) proposed a desperate solution consisting of fighting to the last soldier, while the King and his family were placed in the center of the battlefield surrounded by kegs of gun powder so that at the last moment they are set on fire to avoid the capture of the King and his family by the enemy who would certainly kill them in a humiliating way.

The Migan (executioner and minister of justice) named Landiga O-So-Ofia nodded, as did all the other chiefs and ministers. Then the princes took turn to speak. The first four princes agreed with the opinion expressed by the elders. On the other hand, the youngest, Avissou, proposed to take flight by walking in the river with the water up to chest height. << Half submerged, let's go upstream. After a good walk we will arrive at the shelter of the thickets of Kantomé beyond the falls of Ajarala. Thus, concealed the Ayonous will lose our trace and we will be saved. >>

This is what was done and the Ayonous lost their tracks and withdrew, but encamped in and around the city of Abomey.

The Yoruba will return to the charge later. To avoid the destruction of his army and the entire kingdom, Agadja surrenders to Alafin's army, on the advice of Prince Awissou who is sequestered in Oyo and who will serve as surety for an annuity that Agadja, who became a vassal, will now have to pay each year. The annuity called the Oyo tribute, consisted of a real son of King, 41 young men, 41 maidens, 41 guns, 41 barrels of powder, 41 sacks of cowries, 41 pieces of fabric, and others items. This tribute will remain in place and will stabilize the relations between Oyo and the Danxomè a little until King Guézo the great managed a long time afterwards to defeat Oyo and to stop the payment of this odious tribute.

King AGADJA and the tribute of OYO

The kingdom of Abomey paid a tribute to the kingdom of OYO whose power and authority extended from NIGERIA to the

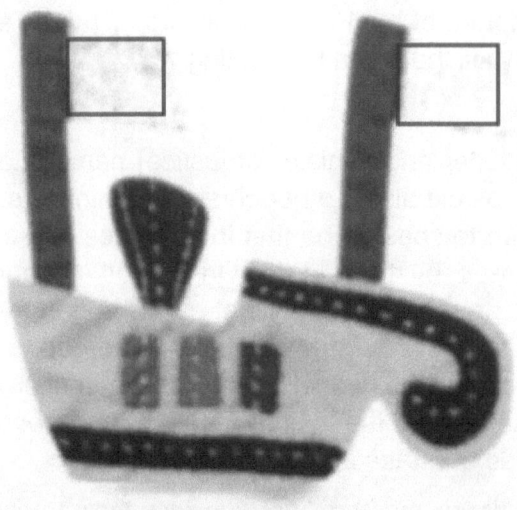

plateau of KETOU and KPEDEKPO. DOSSOU-AGADJA, finding this annoying and too heavy, refused to continue paying it. The Yorubas of OYO launched a strong expedition against Abomey which was quickly captured. AGADJA and the survivors of his army fled to ATAKPAME and found refuge in WEHONOU.

The Yoruba invaded Abomey and settled there. They rejected all negotiations and demanded the head of King AGADJA. The intrepid intractable and powerful Yoruba warriors plunged into the surrounding forest looking for the slightest clue that would allow them to find the traces of the fugitives. They scattered under the lush vegetation, searched every nook and cranny, every bush, every thicket in a very meticulous manner. They were ruthless. Any animal that was discovered was slaughtered. Any reckless, innocent and naive man who ventured around was killed. The shadow of death hovered over the head of every moving soul.

Meanwhile in Abomey, the kingless populations were left to the whims of the Yoruba princes. They were overwhelmed by the harsh chores of fetching water, cooking food, doing laundry and dishes, bathing the Yoruba soldiers and satisfying all their sexual desires.

AGADJA and the bravery of AVOKANLIN

King AGADJA gathered his council. All the parameters indicated the impossibility of the King's return to Abomey. AGADJA would probably have died of shame. He would have committed suicide to avoid the stigma of total defeat. It was imperative to find a solution. The whole council was thinking. AGADJA raised his head and drew everyone's attention to himself. He asked for one valiant volunteer able to pass through the cracks of the relentless Yoruba warriors to go to the palace of King AKABA in Abomey, recover the magic skull of YAHASSE and bring it back to the current king in WEHONOU in ATAKPAME.

A great silence hung over the meeting room for a long time. The fear of certain death froze all those who were present. It was a very risky mission with a low probability of survival. As no one was volunteering, AVOKANLIN son of DANGBALI raised his head and agreed to fulfill the mission. He declared: "I am the vulture which will hover in the air from ATAKPAME to ABOMEY, and whose shadow will frighten the birds. I will bring YAHASSE's head back. >> He listed the items he will need to disguise himself as Yoruba. When everything he asked for was gathered, he dressed himself up right in front of the King, received the King's blessing, and departed. Thanks to his mastery of the Yoruba language and customs, he managed to pass among the enemy soldiers by posing as one of their own. He chatted, ate and sometimes slept among them before reaching his destination.

This is how AVOKANLIN succeeded in its mission and managed to bring back the mysterious head to WEHONOU. AGADJA did some rituals before placing the magic skull on the head of a woman to whom he asked to march in front of the troops in the direction of Abomey. Immediately, a large cloud of bees rose from the magic skull and unfurled in the forest, stinging and chasing the Yoruba invaders. OYO's army was forced to retreat and returned to their kingdom.

AGADJA purified his palace, tidied it up and resettled in his capital city. To reward AVOKANLIN, the King appointed him head of a region going from the borders of DOKON and SEHOUN to the Couffo river, including the town of TANGANDJI. He gave him a throne, a dignitary's hat, a white shirt, a large loincloth, a pair of shoes, a necklace, bracelets, a hammock and a parasol. He nicknamed him ANATOHON.

AVOKANLIN found it abnormal and disrespectful for him to be head of region while his father was still alive and present. So he presented his father with the title and all the awards. DANGBALI (father of AVOKANLIN) left GNIDJAZOUN to settle in AKOUTA and became the first region leader with the title of ANATOHON. Upon DANGBALI's death, his son AVOKANLIN took over and became the second ANATOHON.

The famous gong of the kingdom or the KPANLIN-GAN

Chief AWESSOU could not hide his great satisfaction when he learned of the new knighthood and appointment of his best friend AVOKANLIN. What a happy event! The two friends, who were moreover bound by a blood pact, saw each other very frequently, ate, drank and chatted all the time. They rendered each other many favors and useful services over the years. They had a lot of mutual trust.

In his spare time, AVOKANLIN even helped KPALIN to praise AWESSOU by ringing the gong all around the little palace. He did it willingly very often, so much so that he no longer needed to be followed. He did, however, have a secret objective that he did not reveal to anyone. He could not bear the fact that a mere chief like his friend AWESSOU could have people singing his praise all day long while even the King of Danxomè did not receive such an honor. <<Only King AGADJA deserved this great honor.>> He thought in his mind.

One day, when KPANLIN once again offered him the opportunity to praise AWESSOU, AVOKANLIN ran away with the gong. KPANLIN realized it and went to warn AWESSOU who launched a pursuit with the speed of a gazelle. He caught up with him moments later, grabbed hold of him and knocked him down. AVOKANLIN managed to free himself and the two men continued to fight. The gong had already fallen by the side of the road. The struggle was fierce and the forces equal. At one-point AVOKANLIN pretended to want to gain momentum and come back to the charge; but instead he grabbed the gong and scampered off. The location of the fight between AWESSOU and AVOKANLIN was later named GANHWLITIN. The grass trampled and killed to its core, never grew again in this location, up to this day.

AWESSOU, caught off guard by the tactics of his thief friend, abandoned the pursuit and returned home. AVOKANLIN arrived at King AGADJA's palace, gave him the stolen gong and told him the whole story. Since that time, the populations of DOKON and AKOUTA stopped trusting each other. This is how the habit of praising the kings with the gong started in the royal palaces of Danxomè. The gong praised AGADJA, TEGBESSOU and all the Kings who followed.

KPANLIN put himself at the service of AGADJA. The post of KPANLIN became an institution in the royal court of Danxomè. This was the starting point of an atmosphere of very tense hatred between AVOKANLIN and AWESSOU which cut off all contact with his friend who had become a thief of his gong. AVOKANLIN was extra-careful and took steps to avoid meeting AWESSOU on his way. A few years later, the two died and left their thrones to their heirs AWESSOU AGBODJIHOUN in DOKON and ANATOHON ADJANOU in AKOUTA.

Agadja was a great king. During his reign, the kindom started to trade officially with Europe, and through two seaports: Djékin (Cotonou) and Ouidah. Agadja only came short against the

Yorubas of Oyo. Agadja was also nicknamed the Taker of Boats. He died in 1740 of a brief illness, leaving a much larger Danxome kingdom. East to West, from the Couffo river to the Ouémé river; and South to North, from the Atlantic Ocean to the Mahi territories. Savalou had an agreement with Abomey and retained a relative autonomy.

The children of AGADJA
- King BOSSA AHADE TEGBESSOU
- King GNANSOUNOU KPENGLA
- Prince ZINGAH
- Princess NAGUEZE
- Prince AWISSOU (not to be confused with AWESSOU)
- Other children

Kpalin-gan of the kings (Kpalin and his gong)

Encounter with an European vessel

King Bossa Ahadé TEGBESSOU (1740-1774)

Emblem: dressed buffalo

Motto: Nothing can force the dressed buffalo to remove its tunic.

Awu djé agbo ko bo klonklonglo

The dressed buffalo is difficult to undress. This Emblem alludes to an incident that occurred during his coronation. As part of the proceedings, Tégbessou had to wear his father's tunic for a whole day to show that he was fit to follow in his footsteps. Unbeknown to him, the tunic had been filled with stinging and ticklish leaves that were expected to irritate his skin and make him promptly remove the robe. Tegbessou overcame the ordeal and chose that motto and emblem as a veiled message to whoever wanted to make a fool of him. There are three competing explanations of the names of this king.

(1) Tégbessou, a small plant will grow despite the leaves littering the ground "ama ma gbi gbé no tégbessou"

(2) An oral tradition collected in Abomey (BENIN) from the Tokpo family in November 1991 by Dominique Juhé-Beaulaton indicates that: A prince (àhovi) was sent to Ayotomè (Oyo among the Yorubas); when he left, he took some cola avì, àtakun, àhòwé with him and there he refused to eat anything that was given him for three days. So his hosts said, "If he doesn't want to eat, then send him to weed the yam field." But he did not weed the field and declared: "If you wait for me to weed this yam field, then it will be bushy" (té glé àyonu ton gbo jè na su), hence the name of "Tégbésu" (Tégbessou) selected by prince Bossa Ahadé when he became king.

(3) Some linguists and historians will also interpret the name after the fact as "the yam field is covered with weeds", to recall the alleged end of the King as a hostage in Yoruba country where he was used as a laborer in a field of yams. "Té" being the word in the Fon language for "yam". This cannot be correct since

the facts giving rise to a name cannot come after the name is already in use. Tégbessou's stay in the kingdom of Oyo probably goes back to the time when he was still a prince and was conveyed there as part of the annual tribute that the kingdom of Danxomè had to pay to Oyo and which had to include an authentic prince in addition to the slaves and other merchandise.

Panegyric of Tegbessou in Fongbe and in English

Tegbesu awu je agbokò
Tegbessou, the dressed buffalo

Xâde, Axâde awu wè jè agbokò
O Axâde, the buffalo is dressed

Awu wê je agbokò bo koklo vê ku e, koklo ve ku e
To remove this garment worn by the buffalo, you first have to kill him, you have to kill him first.

Awu e më de do, më de do, Axâde, awu kò yi awamë
This garment, Ahadé, already has it in his arms

Zanu Hünö hutò
The one who killed Hünö chief of Za. (This chief of the region of Cana had criticized the King of Abomey for wanting to build his mother's temple in his nose.)

Awôtï kpanu zanëto
The one who cut off the noses of the people of Za. (It took six campaigns to totally defeat the people of Za. After conquering the area, he cut the nose of some of the soldiers made prisoners.)

B'agala dele
Example of courage

Mama Degwe lo adetò
The intrepid Mama Degwë (magical name of Tegbessou)

After taking power, Tegbessou arrested his elder brother Zingah, suspected of conspiracy and sedition against the king, and had him drowned by throwing him overboard from a canoe in the Ouidah lagoon.

It is Tégbéssou who in 1741 will become uncontested master of Ouidah and make it an effective territory of Abomey. He will appoint the first Yovogan (a name that would later become famous under Guézo when the post was held by "Chacha" Francisco de Souza). The Yovogan is a minister or emissary of the King who stays in Ouidah and takes care of trade with the Europeans. With Chacha (who was a personal and sincere friend of Guézo), the position took on more importance and became almost a kind of vice-king or viceroy or prime-minister.

Hodonou was the first Yovogan Tegbessou appointed. History will fortuitously link this Hodonou with one of my ancestors ADJINA NONGLOKPO MEDALI GBAGUIDI who gave Hodonou the formula to finally have a male child and future heir. This connection forever changed the destinies of the two men and their descendants. For more information, refer to the book < **Kings, Princes, Slaves and Nobles** > by the same author.

Tegbessou (like Adandozan decades later) refused to pay the full tribute to the Yoruba of Oyo in the later years of his rule. As a punishment, Cana and Abomey were set ablaze by the Yoruba and a tax collector ambassador was imposed on the kingdom to ensure the regularity of the tribute payment.

The children of TEGBESSOU

- Prince ADJOKPALO
- Other children

The Army of Danxomè repels a French naval attack (Illustration, 1892, Petit Journal)

King Yansounou KPINGLA (1774-1789)

Emblem: a bird (sparrow), a stone in the water and a gun
Motto: The restless bird attacks other birds.

Born: 1735 (Abomey). Death: 1789 (Abomey)

"sinmé kpingla ma sin avivo"

The stone in the water is not afraid of the cold.

This means: that the King does not fear any enemy, like a stone in water. This eloquently evokes the adversities he had to face.

Panegyric of Kpingla in Fongbe and in English

Axòsu Sïmëkpë

O King you are like a stone in the water

(Strong name of Kpengla, taken from the legend surrounding his birth. Tradition indeed reports that Yansounou (the future Kpengla), son of Naye Tchayi, had been taken from his mother and abandoned in a stream. The water stream cannot harm a stone.)

Aladanu Adimulavi Sïmëkpë

O Sîmèkpë, son of Adimula of Allada

(Adimula or Ademola is a Yoruba name of Tegbessou, father of Kpingla)

Xwenu do do xomëvi Sïmëkpë

O Sïmëkpë, son of the walls of this palace

(Allusion to the difficulties that Kpëgla encountered during his enthronement: the Migan would have prohibited him from entering the royal palace

Sïmëkpë ma j'avivo

Stone in water does not fear the cold

Kudohü bo de ma du

Nobody dance to the rhythm of death

Xwêda axòsu Agbamu hutò

He who killed Agbamu, King of Xwêda

(Agbamou had taken the xwêda throne at the expense of his rival Yë by taking advantage of Tegbessou's death and attempted to rebel against Abomey's rule over Savi and Ouidah. Kpingla crushed his troops and killed him.)

Kla kpodo Jëgë kpo hutò

He who killed Kla and Jëgë (two xwêda chiefs who were twins.)

Abogwe më nu Sitò hutò
He who killed Sitò, leader of the people of Abogoué (near Allada)

Sitò sa daxo de wulitò
He who captured the great and cunning Sitò

B'agaia dele
Example of courage

Dada awadonu lo adëtô
The intrepid but accessible King

The pronunciation is "Kpingla" but both "Kpengla" and "Kpingla" are correct spellings. It's the same for "Guézo". "Ghézo" and sometimes "Gezo", as well as other names of Kings and people.

Brother of Tegbessou, Kpengla succeeded him and crushed the revolt led by Agbamou the Houeda King of Savi, and had him executed.

Kpengla encountered strong resistance during his campaigns against the Mahi, Dassa, and Bariba kingdoms. Kpengla dominated Savalou but in the name of the previous links between the two kingdoms, he did not destroy it. However, he appointed their next ruler and kept them as a vassal territory.

Kpengla complied with the demands of Oyo's tribute. The oral tradition relates an interesting story that took place in the year that Prince Agonglo was chosen as the crown prince to accompany the items to be delivered to the King of Oyo, during the reign of Kpengla. Refer to the King Agonglo section for more information about those events.

The children of KPENGLA

- AGONGLO
- Other children

King AGONGLO (1789-1797)

Emblem: the ronier palm tree (Borassus aethiopum) and the pineapple

Motto: Lightning strikes the palm tree, but never the ronier palm tree.

So je de b'agon glo.

This Motto alludes to the lightning incident he escaped, as well as all the obstacles he escaped even before ascending to the throne. At the beginning of Agonglo's reign, he had to face the most devious intrigues. This sentence was said to have been uttered following an accident which nearly cost him his life: during a ceremony for Xèbioso (god of lightning), lightning fell on the palm tree under which the King was standing; it was of course thought that the priests of Xèbioso were no strangers to this and may have made an attempt on the life of the king.

The misinterpretation of King AGONGLO's Emblem

It is true that the ronier palm tree is less prevalent in Benin today than it was in the 18th century. But the King's name alludes to the ronier palm tree. The ronier is the most important element of the Emblem, along with the pineapple. Unfortunately, in many books and articles, commentators only talk about pineapples. This error has been repeated almost everywhere by Beninese and Western authors, both in French and in English, including by wise men like Jean Pliya.

There is no confusion regarding the Fon version: So je de b'agon glo. Three vegetable essences bear the name of "agon" in the Fon language: coconut (agon-kè), ronier (agon-té or agon-téglé) and pineapple (agon-de). The coco is excluded de facto because the coconut palm is known for its tendency to attract rather than repel lightning, due to its size and the humidity of its trunk. The ronier is known by the populations and the ancients for its ability to ward off or not suffer from lightning. The ronier is an endogenous plant which was known for a long time in

Danxomè. The ronier is therefore retained. What about pineapple?

Pineapple belongs to the category of vegetable essences imported from America and is not endogenous to Danxomè. But when did it come to West Africa? The first pineapple plants would have been introduced during the reign of Agonglo who strongly promoted them, just like his son will much later promote the oil palm tree. This is also why pineapple became his Emblem. The popularity of the pineapple, and perhaps the complexity of the representation of the ronier, made some historians, graphic designers and dyers even ignore the ronier palm tree altogether and invent elaborate explanations of the connection between the pineapple plant and the King.

The most reliable source for the Danxome Kings symbol is their assin. When the King dies, the best blacksmiths in the kingdom work together with the sages and custodians of knowledge to craft an assin that perfectly materializes the King's story and emblem. The following photo of Agonglo's assin dates from the 1970s and was first printed by Jean Pliya. We can clearly see the two elements: the ronier palm tree and the pineapple. This definitely settles the puzzle.

Photo of King Agonglo's Assin

Panegyric of Agonglo in Fongbe and in English

So je de b'agon glo (bis)
Lightning falls on the palm tree, but spares the rönier tree (bis)

Axazo, zo bada
Boiling drink, amazing fire

B'axa na
Dangerous drink

Cici li ta
Crackling fire

Gbowelenu Ajoyô hutò
He who killed Ajoyo of Gbowélé
(Gbowélé is a hill of the Mahi region. This Ajayô was allied to the family of the famous Yaxèze (Yahasse) defeated by Akaba)

Sïgwïdï gbatò
He who destroyed Sïgwïdï (Mahi village)

Xêbêco hutò
He who killed Xëbêco (Mahi chief)

B'agala dele
Example of courage

Sojë de b'agôglo lö adetö
The intrepid Agonglo is spared by the lightning that falls on the tree.

One year, Prince Agonglo was chosen as the crown prince to accompany the tribute of Oyo. But before his departure, his mother had secretly given him a magic calabash. Although he was part of the tribute and thus expected to become the property of the kingdom of Oyo, the prince was treated better than the slaves and was supposed to become a citizen of Oyo. He therefore received the characteristic scars of the Yoruba of this region since he was never supposed to return to his family in Abomey.

Later, upon returning to Danxomè, Agonglo had a particular style of hat made to hide his cheeks, preventing his subjects from discovering the scars inherited from his stay in captivity in Oyo. This kind of hat will be popularized much later by Gbèhanzin who wore a similar model during his famous meeting with General Dodds and the French troops in Goho.

During his reign Agonglo attempted multiple reforms which pleased the people. He reduced taxes, especially those on trade in Ouidah. He improved the conditions of detention of prisoners. He did not hesitate to distribute some of his too many wives to his best soldiers to motivate and reward them. Agonglo's troops defeated the Mahi of Gboweto and the Ouatchis.

Agonglo, feeling his end near, consulted the Fâ to designate his successor, it is Guézo the younger who was appointed. But he was too young: it was not until 21 years later that he took power by force, after the tumultuous reign of his big brother ADANDOZAN.

The children of AGONGLO

- King ADANDOZAN MADOGUGU
- King GAKPE GUEZO
- ALAVO
- ADOUKONOU
- SINCOUTIN
- ASSOGBAOU
- TOFFA (not to be confused with the king of Porto-Novo)
- AHEHEHINNOU
- AHOKPE
- Others

Photo of a bas-relief of Guézo's Adjalala

King ADANDOZAN Madogugu (1797-1818)

Emblem: a woven mat

Motto: "Adandozan ma gnon fli"

Anger spreads its mat and no one can roll it up. I am angry with the Yoruba and no one can force me to come to terms with them.

A bas-relief decoration is dedicated to the King of the Yoruba of Oyo. It depicts a seated monkey with a bloated belly which has its mouth full and is still holding an ear of corn. This monkey represents the Alafin of Oyo because Adandozan considers him a greedy animal that can only feed on the hard work of others kingdoms. The regency of Adandozan was important. He fought against the tribute of the Yoruba of Oyo.

Adandozan had long been removed from the official list and sacred history of the Kings of Danxomè following a strict edict promulgated by his successor, brother and rival Gakpé (Guézo the Great). If recently the work of researchers and historians has made it possible to resuscitate his memory, Adandozan remains taboo within the walls of Danxomè and in Abomey to this day.

Adandozan was a magus with supernatural powers and endowed with extraordinary political intelligence. This is why even once dethroned, he was not put to death, but received the privilege of instructing the most important princes of the kingdom. He counted Behanzin and Goutchili (both future rulers of the kingdom) among his illustrious pupils.

He was ahead of his time, realizing early on that the slave trade was negative for the kingdom (and for the continent) and that certain ancestral traditions (such as burying a sovereign with his wives, servants and expensive belongings) were barbaric and should be abolished.

It's not his ideas (generally correct, wise and truthful) that made other members of the royal family and the citizens of the kingdom, despise him. It is the methods he used to convince everyone else or force his viewpoint on them.

To show the aberration of the slave trade, he added princesses and even queens to the usual roster of war prisoners, convicts and captured people who were usually sold as slaves. One of these queens he sold was the mother of the future King Ghézo: this act created one of the strongest enmities and rivalries in the history of Danxomè. His opposition to the slave trade also created bad blood between him and the influential Portuguese merchant and governor Francisco de Souza Chacha who freed Gakpé (future Ghézo) from the clutches of Adandozan and later aided him in his coup to gain power.

To demonstrate his occult powers, he once set out to correctly guess the sex of the children some pregnant women were carrying. To verify the veracity of his prediction, he had the mothers disemboweled in order to examine the genitals of the babies, thereby causing the deaths of both mothers and children.

He sometimes offered his opponents and bandits to hungry hyenas and watched their agony when they were being devoured alive. He sometimes made two old men fight seriously with sticks on pain of death (if they refused) and laughed at their clumsiness. These incidents did not please the people and contributed to the King's bad reputation.

If the death-fights of the gladiators of ancient Rome and the habit of feeding prisoners to lions and other wild beasts were among the popular games of this cradle of European civilization, these games were for the sadistic amusement of the people as a whole and not for the sole pleasure of the king, as was the case with Adandozan. Not to imply that the roman practices were less barbaric. These things are really horrible and deplorable, but it is important to give a historical context so that the reader understands that other nations around the world also went through these dark phases.

An Australian tourist asked me once in New York in an elevator where I was from. When I told him that I was from Benin, he asked with a smirk if this was not the country where people were beheaded in the past. In retrospect, I should have asked him if this is the first question he usually asks when he meets a French or a Spaniard. It is indeed in France that political prisoners and opponents were regularly guillotined in the 17th and 18th centuries. It was in Spain that the Inquisition took place and women were burned alive for their beliefs. These things were happening either in the same period or just before the period when the Kings of Danxomè had some prisoners' heads cut off. Moreover, this kind of nonsense continues to occur today in countries like Saudi Arabia, which the governments of the lesson-givers still consider as their important ally or partner and do not criticize. At the time of this writing, beheadings are still legal and routinely done in Saudi Arabia.

Adandozan died in 1861, decades after his reign ended in 1818.

The children of ADANDOZAN
I do not yet have information on the descendants of Adandozan who mostly changed their family name to avoid reprisals.

Illustration of King Guézo 1

Illustration of King Guézo 2

Photo of one of the trônes of King Guézo

King GUEZO, the Great (1818-1858)
Gakpe Gbalangbe Zedoko Ghézo (Guézo)

Emblem: a jug with many holes, and a buffalo

Motto: If each of you, sons of this nation, can plug a hole with your finger, the jug will hold the water. The mighty buffalo crosses the country and nothing can stop or oppose it.

"gé dé zo ma si gbé"

Despite its flamboyance no cardinal (bird) can set the bush on fire (so my enemies are powerless against me)

"agbo do glo non zré to"

the buffalo, which has become powerful, crosses the country without encountering obstacles.

I am the buffalo that crosses the country and nothing can stop me.

Mural showing King Guézo

Panegyric of Guézo in Fongbe and in English

Axòsu gbalägbe

O shining King (and renowned hunter)

Adäzü litò Gbalägbe

O Gbalangbé who erected the tumulus of courage (This tumulus is still visible in the Bëcon-Hounli district. It is there that the King, when he returns from his military campaigns, announces his victories and pronounces the statements which are to remain in the historical anals of the oral tradition.)

Ayòxwan füto Gbalägbe

O Gbalangbé who started the war against Oyo (Guézo undertook several campaigns against the powerful Yoruba kingdom of Oyo, to which Dahomey paid a large tribute annually.)

Gbalägbe ma bu do gbexomê

O Gbalangbé who never gets lost in the bush

Akpo wê ci gedehüsu b'ë yi xë do

It is to dispel his boredom that the great kapok tree calls the birds. (The great kapok tree is one of the King's emblems.)

Kpò do gbe bò se ma gö

When the panther is in the bush, the civet does not venture nearby. (The panther symbolizes the King, and at the same time the founding ancestor of the dynasty and the Fon people.)

Kpò dò se ku na gö wo

The panther said she would kill the civet if she ever sees it.

Avo gbè nu xo bò sevola yi xo

The dog refuses to bark, and the antelope offers to do it.

Bo ni axòsu-gbodo

And you are great king

Maxi Hüjroto gbatò

He who destroyed the Mahi country of Houndjro (Important victory commemorated by the installation of the main market of Abomey: the market of Houndjro-to.)

Anago Lefulefu gbatò

He who destroyed the Nago village of Lefulefu (or Refurefu, conquered during the first campaign against Abëokuta around 1843)

Ayònu Acade hutò

He who killed Atchade of Oyo. (Atchade was the top general of Oyo's army.)

Acadesi Agbâlï wulitò

He who kidnapped Agbâlï, the wife of general Atchade

B'agaia dele

Example of courage

Dâxomë lo azomètò lo adètò

The intrepid who was repeatedly master of Danxomè.

(King Guézo was crowned a first time by his father Agonglo, and a second time by himself after overthrowing Adandozan.)

Axòsu zekete

O King that cannot be uprooted. (That is to say, nobody cannot overthrow him. Gezo was indeed very strong physically and passed for an excellent warrior. He was also chief of the military)

Zekete ma sedo do lo xwe

The one who cannot be removed from his father's house

Nu kë ne kë ne ma xa do gboklemê

We find all kinds of food in the mouth of the pig

Gboklemê ma je vò

The mouth of the pig is never empty

Kpla kaca ma nò kple zùkò

Even with a rake you cannot remove all the garbage

Ko ji adu ma le fô
If the tooth is damaged, the mind is not

So kèhû ma le jokpe
Lightning does not attack stone

(The stone here represents the King.)

Loko naki ma d'axa
The wood of the iroko tree does not make noise

Kpakpa d'axä ma fio zë
The cries of the duck do not burn the cooking pot

Maxi Kpo gbatò
He who destroyed the Mahi village of Kpo

Kpo'xòsu Cahu hutò
He who killed Cahu, chief of the Mahi village of Kpo

Canò wulitò
The one who seized Cano

(Cano, Biogo, Bina, Ajami, and Kakatrika were various chiefs of the Mahi people.)

Biogo kpo Bina hutò
He who killed Biogo and Bina

Ajami, Kakatrika hutò
He who killed Ajami and Kakatrika

B'agala dele
Example of courage

Aladanu Gakpe lo adëto
The intrepid Gakpé from Allada

(Gakpé was the name that Guézo had before he was King. Literally, Gakpé means "the arrival of the appointed day." Azan kpe bo Ga kpé. Guézo's princely name therefore expressed an idea of revenge on his brother Adandozan.)

Photo of King Guézo's Adjalala

Details of King Guézo's Adjalala

Ghézo was called by some historians, the Danhomean Attila. Jean Pliya added the qualifier "The Great" to his name because he was comparable to both Louis XIV and Alexander the Great in majesty.

Prince Gakpé, is exiled in Cana (Kanan) since the time his brother Adandozan took power, and survives by hunting and selling game (wild meat). Still considering him a threat, his brother had him arrested and put him under permanent surveillance.

Thanks to the help of supporters living in Abomey and of Chacha De Souza, he managed to escape from house arrest and settled in Ouidah where, being protected by Portugal, he could no longer be reached directly by the King his brother Adandozan. His mother however is unlucky and is sold into slavery by Adandozan. Later when he became King, Guezo went to great lengths to try to find her in Brazil and brought her back. His main wife Agoyi Sindolé, the future Queen Zognidi, narrowly escapes the same fate when she is luckily recognized and freed before her group of future slaves embarked from Ouidah to depart for America.

Agoyi then settled in Ouidah alongside her husband. Under the influence of Chacha De Souza, Agoyi and Gakpé baptized themselves into Catholicism and celebrated their marriage in the chapel of Ouidah. Agoyi takes the Christian first name of Francesca. Both are educated and study the political and economic organization of the colony of Brazil, the country of Portugal and other European nations. All this information will help King Guézo later in his management and transformation of the kingdom.

As retaliation against Chacha, Adandozan refuses to reimburse him for his commercial debts. When Chacha arrives in Abomey to protest, he is arrested by the king. Just like Chacha did for him before, Gakpé also helps Chacha escape from prison in Abomey.

In 1818, Gakpé overthrows his cruel and fanciful brother Adandozan and takes the name of Guézo. Big and strong (like a buffalo) since one day according to legend, he killed with his own hands a wild buffalo that was terrorizing a village.

The coup of 1818 was a very interesting military operation. Adandozan covers his territory very well and has an efficient and vigilant information services (surveillance and secret services), so it will take a lot of tact and creativity for the operation to be planned quietly and executed successfully. Various scenarios are studied and evaluated. Agoyi Francesca Sindolé, Gakpé's wife proposes that former members of the military corps of the Amazons (whom Adandozan in his hasty reforms had hitherto ignored), be used. Only women could enter the capital Abomey with goods without attracting the attention of the very sharp guards. So it made sense that the Amazons could enter by posing as traders or peasants.

Chacha provides the weapons and provisions. Agoyi assisted the Amazons in their disguise and in their preparation. Gakpé, who knows the capital and the palace better than anyone else, takes care of the tactical and military details. The operation is carried out as planned and is a runaway success without much bloodshed, thanks to the decision of the ministers and generals serving under Adandozan to endorse and recognize the new king. Perhaps they were also fed up by the authoritarian drifts of Adandozan, and remembered the initial wishes expressed by the deceased King Agonglo (father of both Adandozan and Guezo). Much of the elite backed the new King and attended his installation.

With affable and dignified manners, of fair complexion and handsome face, the great Guézo was a man of war, diplomat, sage, protector of the arts, and great economist. Under his reign, the country is reorganized, as well as the administration and public functions. The kingdom is divided into provinces with governors responding to the Méhou (Prime Minister). The governors follow the orders received, give the visas for entry into the kingdom, levy taxes on general merchandise and palm oil, the cultivation of which took on an industrial scale.

After the slave trade was outlawed by the British, taxes on goods and revenues from palm oil became the main sources of income for the royal treasury. All the products of the royal plantations are sold by the King's merchants. Guézo increases the number of customs posts on the roads, and the number of duties and taxes levied in the markets.

Local chiefs are accountable and also take care of local justice. Ghézo assigns to his relatives and trustworthy members of the royal family, positions of deputy to the great dignitaries in order to keep an eye on their management. So basically a competent technocrat is appointed to lead each position regardless of royal blood but a prince is appointed as second in command to keep an eye on the leader and report back to the king.

The royal brides keep the keys to the palace stores. The King gives public hearings and dispenses justice. The entrance to the palace was architecturally designed to be low in order to force visitors to bend, lower themselves and greet the King in that position.

In front of his building in Singbodji Square, the king had sumptuous ceremonies and festivities organized annually, often with multiple human sacrifices. These sacrificed humans are traditionally considered as the kingdom's messengers to the deceased Kings and ancestors in the Hereafter. They are tasked to inform them of the living's obedience and deference to them, and the smooth running of the kingdom.

The army becomes professional with structures comparable to those of European armies. This allows Danxome to compete with other African armies equipped by Great Britain, such as Oyo's army. The Danxome troops are equipped with spears, sabers, rifles and cannons. Military maneuvers and physical exercises are carried out regularly.

Ghézo organizes the Amazons into formal military units on par with male military units, with the assistance of Queen ZOGNIDI, his wife. They have uniforms and weapons, and they are used especially for military assaults and surprise attacks. For example they fought valiantly in Abéokouta where they distinguished themselves. They were commanded by their own leaders, captains and others who were also women.

History fully recognizes the prowess of King GUEZO in the field of agricultural production and food processing. The strategist who planned and oversaw the execution of Danxomè's agricultural policy during GUEZO's glorious years was none other than my ancestor, the Minister of Agriculture and Trade KOUDANOU TOKPO.

A modern economy is developing. There is an increase in the cultivation of palm oil, with strict rules. TOKPO, Minister of Agriculture, must enforce them and thus ensure that the heads of all those who dare to cut down a palm tree without authorization be cut off. When a child is born, a Palm tree is planted. Coconut, tobacco, and various other food crops are developed.

After the Great Famine of 1848, Ghézo advocated for the mass-production of agricultural items imported from Brazil such as cassava, soft corn, bananas, peanuts, okra, tomatoes and orange trees. The king appoints intendants to supervise all these plantations. Industrial transformation also took off with the improvement of copper smelting and metallurgy techniques. A textile industry was also developed.

Europe now in full industrialization needs a lot of raw materials including palm oil. The kingdom exchanges palm oil for trinkets, glass beads, copper bracelets, necklaces, handkerchiefs, fabrics, barrels of powders, weapons, liquors and others goods.

In 1851 Ghézo was the first king of Danxomè to make an international act as a modern ruler: he signed a treaty of friendship and trade with the President of the second French republic. For a fee that France was expected to pay to Danxome, the kingdom promised to grant protection to the French traders and their properties.

In 1823, Guezo attacked the Yoruba and liberated his kingdom from the Oyo tribute paid annually since 1732 (the last decade of Agadja's reign) to the Yoruba kingdom of Oyo. Each year, the

Danxomè was required to send forty-one men including at least one crown prince, forty-one women, forty-one oxen, forty-one guns, and so on, a long list of things in quantity of forty-one each. That tribute lasted for 91 years in total before it was stopped.

Reinvigorated by his victory over Oyo, Guezo wanted to conquer all the other Yoruba kingdoms of present-day Nigeria. Regular raids are organized against Gbadagry with success. But his military failures against Abéokuta darkens the end of his reign. During a return from the campaign against the Egba town, near Kétou in Ekpo, he was wounded by a poisoned arrow shot by a young man who fled the scene. This injury will be fatal.

List of the children of GUEZO

- King BADOHOUN GBINGNI KINIKINI Glèlè
- HEGLABE
- ALINWANOU
- FIOGBE
- NAN GBELI-TON
- GUEZODJE
- KEDIFI
- YAMONGBE AGBOBADJI
- AZINFAN
- AHOSSIN
- ADJAGBONISSI
- NOUDAYI
- DAKO
- HOUDOHOUE
- NAGNI
- Other children

Origin of the names AGBANGNIZOUN and AHINADJE

AGBANGNIZOUN = AGBANLIN ZOUN = an antelope forest where king Guezo used to go for hunting.

AHINADJE = NOUN ASSE HO E DO N'DE O, AHI NAWA DJE DO FI = "If you accept to marry me, your descendants will be so numerous that this place will be like a market place." King GUEZO made this declaration to a lovely young lady from the house of FOLI whom he met. AHINADJE became not only the nickname of the lady but also of the place.

From Agadja to Ghézo the goal was to consolidate the territory acquired by Agadja, to free the kingdom from the tribute imposed by the King of Oyo, and to enrich the country by capturing prisoners for labor on the royal plantations and to be sold as slaves. Kings Tégbessou, Kpengla, Agonglo and Adandozan tried to resist the Yorouba of Oyo, but it was Guézo who defeated them.

Note from a visitor to the palace of Ghézo

« We walk towards him, hats off; he gets up, takes a few steps in front of us, approaches us, and after having successively shaken hands in European fashion, he invites us to sit down in armchairs arranged in front of his throne. There was something really impressive about the appearance of the assembly.

To the King's right stood 600 female members of his bodyguard squatting Turkish-style on rugs in perfect stillness, guns between their legs. Behind them a darker line the elephant huntresses, dressed in brown cloth and armed with long rifles with blackened barrels.

To his left the women of the seraglio of about two hundred, some barely teenagers, others in all the brilliance and development of black beauty, some already of a certain age, but all covered with rich fabrics of silk.

Standing behind the royal armchair, three or four favorites as well as the general-in-chief of the Amazons. Before the King, on the steps of the platform where his chair had been placed, his son and the principal ministers were kneeling.

On a table set between him and us, we were served refreshments contained in crystal bottles and a rich liquor of European origin. »

End of quote

King Glèlè Kinikini (1858-1889)
Badohoun Gbingni Ahogla Togodo Bassagla Delele

Emblem: lion

Motto: The lion cub begins to sow terror among its enemies as soon as its teeth have grown.

No being can lift the earth or a field (so no one can uproot me)

Photo of King Glèlè's Adjalala (after restauration)

King Glèlè

Panegyric of Glèlè in Fongbe and in English

Axòsu Glêlë
O King Glêlë

Dâxomè'xòsu Gêlêlè
O Glêlè, King of Dahomey

As'vii e adatò Gêlêlè ma no ze
O courageous master Glêlë whom nobody can lift or uproot

E na ze b'è glo
Nobody can lift or uproot you

E kple na zi dodo b'è glo
They gather to bring you down but they fail

E do mi na xo b'adida
That's why we will carry you together

Xë ma xo agbo'tà b'è glo
No bird will mess with a fiery buffalo. It is impossible

Agovèsuvi Gêlêlè b'è glo
Nobody will mess with Glêlë, it is impossible

Na ce gbo bo ci Gêlêlè
Nobody will dare mess with Glêlë

Anago Dumê gbatò
He who conquered the Nago town of Doumé

Niekàtaku hutò
He who killed Niekàtaku (chief of Doumé)

Axòsu kololo
O great King

We dede kololo ma nò miâ
Be careful if you approach him

Goni, goni, ni mo nò bë
Hide if you hear him coming

Anago Dumè gbatò
He who conquered the Nago town of Doumé

Niekàtaku hutò
He who killed Niekàtaku

Axòsu kololo
O great King

N'xòmla we lade
I praised you, ô King

N'xòmlà we as'wi e
I praised you, ô my master

Axosu Gèlele
O King Glële

As'vii e adatò Gëlëlè ma fio ze
O courageous master Glêlë whom nobody can lift or uproot

E na ze b'ë glo
Nobody can lift or uproot you

E kple na zï dodo b'ê glo
They gather to bring you down but they fail

E do mi na xo b'adida
That's why we will carry you together

Axòsu Jezo
O King Jèzo

(Jèzo = Rare pearl that triumphs over the test of fire. It's an allusion to his mom's nickname "Jè nana xo zognidi" and to his own triumph over fire. First when he was a baby and a stepmother tried to assassinate him by setting his room on fire. Two babies were in the room at the time, two princes and future kings. The stepmother thought she grabbed her own baby when in fact she unknowingly rescued the other baby. Next, after Glele became king, his palace was burnt down by embittered descendants of Adandozan who were still fuming over how Guezo kicked Adandozan from power.)

Dâxomê'xosu Jèzo
O Jëzo, King of Danxomè

As'wi e adatò Jêzo mò nò ci wë
O master, courageous Jêzo that no one can extinguish

Anago Dumë gbatò
He who destroyed the Nago town of Doumé

Niekàtaku hutò
He who killed Niekàtaku

Axòsu kololo
O great King

We dede kololo ma no mia
Be careful if you approach him

Goni, goni, ni mo no bè
Hide if you hear him coming

Akata'xòsu azua
O king who ascended on Akata's mound (This mound is between Mono and Allada on the edge of Tchi)

Tri so gbatò
He who conquered the town of Tri and so many mountains (The mountains of the Mahi kingdom)

Baba tri nätö
He who defeated the ruler of Tri

Sonu wulitò
He who captured Sonu (a king of the Mahi)

Sosi da nu Aladanu Gakpeto
And gave his wife to the Gakpe of Allada

(He sacrificed the the Mahi queen, wife of the defeated king to his dad. Gakpe is another name of King Guézo, father of King Glele. Allada is the origin land of the Fon before their settlement of the Zou region. Allada is also the celestial land where the souls of the kings of Danxome return to after their death.)

Aladanu Baduze
Baduze, descendant of Allada

(Before becoming King, Glèlè was named Badohoun which is abbreviated as Baduze, Badou and Badu)

Baduze'bo

Praises to Baduze

Nu wa atï bò kä ma ko

When the tree is in trouble, the liana does not make fun of it (The tree is the king. The liana represents the king's enemy. The liana depends on the tree for its own life and sustenance.)

Agbo lì mèsu mêto kli kpezo

Order has been restored to the land

So je gbe bò Blu jo kö

The warrior Blu has missed his shot and stamps his feet

Gälinu ma ku trò tu

He will have enough time to reload his gun

N'xömlä we lade

I praise you, ô King

N'xòmla we as'wi e

I praise you, ô master

Axòsu Gèlele

O King Glëlê

Anago Dumë gbatò

He who destroyed the Nago town of Doumé

Niekataku hutò

He who killed Niekàtaku

Caga gbatò

He who destroyed the Yoruba city of Ishaga to avenge Ghezo

Caga'xòsu Bakoko hutò

He who killed Bakoko, King of Ishaga

B'agala dele

Example of courage

Gbetïsa Jëgbeto lo adëto

The intrepid king-warrior to whom the Djègbë mound is dedicated

(When he was still a prince, Glèlè lived in the Djègbë district of Abomey. It was there that a palace had been built for him, as was customary. We can still see the mound erected by Guézo in honor of his son Badohûn's hunting deeds and war exploits.)

Glèlè agreed to give Cotonou to the French by a treaty signed on May 19, 1868. But we will never know if the interpreters accurately explained to the king, the content of the paper he was signing. Two decades later, his son Gbèhanzin denounced this treaty and wanted to void it, but France ignored his request.

Glèlè died in 1889, leaving an innumerable offspring, just as he had promised: an offspring so important that from then on, nothing will happen in Danxomè without their involvement.

List of the children of Glèlè, adult male and alive at the time of his death

1. ABIDO
2. ADJAHA-FINGBE
3. ADJAHO
4. ADJATOUN
5. AGAYA-AVOKAN
6. AGBIDINOUKOUN
7. AGBOHO-BESSOUGLA
8. AGOSSAVI
9. AHANHANZO
10. AHI-FIYOGBETON
11. AHO-DOBA
12. AHO-TANGANTEVE
13. AHOVO
14. AIGBAGBA
15. AINONKPO
16. AIWENONSE
17. AKOUTOUSSI
18. AKPADO
19. AKPANIAKOU
20. AKPOKPO
21. ASSOGBA-GANHA
22. ASSOGBA-HOUNTO
23. ASSOGBA-KINON
24. ATIGBEKAN
25. AVALIGBE-DJAMY
26. AVALIGBE-HANGANSOU
27. AZEHOUNGBO
28. AZONMADAGBE
29. BAI
30. BINON-YI

31. BOSSOU-GNIGLAKPON
32. BOSSOU-VI
33. DADAGLO
34. DAH-NONGBE
35. DAH-GBETO
36. DAKO-AHEHEHINNOUTON
37. DAKO-AKOTE
38. DAKO-CHOCOLAT
39. DAKO-KPELELI ZADO
40. DAKO-MEWAN
41. DAKOHOUIN-DJASSOU
42. DAKOSSI-LAN
43. DEGAN
44. DESSOU
45. DJIDAGBAGBA
46. DJISSONON
47. DJOFOUNOU
48. DJOKODJE
49. DOHIN-SIN
50. DOHOUNBIDJI
51. DOKOGUI-YIN
52. DOSSOU-CONFITURE
53. DOSSOU-DJOKPEZE
54. DOSSOU-HLAGBA
55. DOTE-GA
56. EGBO
57. FAGBADJI
58. FINGBE
59. GANGBLA-HIN
60. **Gbêhanzin-AIJRE KONDO (King BEHANZIN)**
61. GBEMAVLEKPO
62. GBLANGBE
63. GBOHAIDA ZINDEHA
64. GLEDJE
65. GOUNYSOZAN
66. **GOUTCHILI (King AGOLI-AGBO)**
67. GUEZO-WEZON
68. HLIHO-AKODO
69. HOUEDOKOHO
70. HOUESSOU-WATRA
71. HOUNSEDO
72. HOUNTIN-TOGBAN
73. KAKAI
74. KESSI
75. KODJADOU
76. KPAKATCHA
77. KPADJAGLA-ZADOTON
78. KPADJAGLA-VOU
79. KPAKPASSOU
80. KPANNA-AGBAHOUNDO
81. KPEDJEKOU
82. KPELI (KPELELI)
83. KPOGBOZAN
84. KPOGLA

85. KPOKPODO-KPOSSOU
86. KPOZINHOUE
87. LANDEDO-ADJAGLE
88. LANGANFIN
89. LEHOUNKON
90. MEHOUSSI
91. MELE (TOKPA-MELE)
92. MIGANSI
93. NAOUFOU
94. NOUBIGBE
95. OUANITO-ZINHA
96. SAGBADJOU
97. SASSE-KPAKPALOULOU
98. SESSOU-DAN
99. SESSOU-GOUGBE
100. SESSOU-NOUDO
101. SINDOGBE
102. SOFFOUN
103. SOGLO
104. TCHANKPANAN
105. TCHIKITIMI-BOSSOU
106. TOHA
107. TOKPA-DOLAKAN
108. TOKPA-HLOWANSOU
109. TOMANAGA
110. TONONDJI
111. TOSSA-DJOKODJE
112. TOSSI
113. TOSSOU-AGANSA
114. TOSSOU-VOHE
115. TOYE-OU
116. VIGNIGBE
117. WEKELIVO
118. YADICLE
119. YEDONOU
120. YETINKPETO
121. ZODEHOUGAN
122. ZOTON-BOBO

I continue to complete this non-exhaustive list because the daughters of Glèlè and some children who died before the king are not included.

Danxomè Soldier vs Oyo Soldier

Letter of King Glélé to Dom Louis the 1st, King of Portugal

Sicamè Palace, July 16, 1887

Regarding the protectorate: when in August 1885 Juliao F. de Souza and Dr Meyrelles Leite came here, I was at war and I sent my son Coundo, Crown Prince of my throne, to speak to Juliao in order to agree with the Portuguese so that they come to trade in Ajuda, in exchange for workers bought by the colonists; and in July 1886, when Major Antonio D. da Silva Curado came on mission, I spoke to him about the same affair of the merchants, and the treaty made by Juliao and Meyrelles never came to my knowledge until very recently. These are things that I never ordered and none of my ministers are aware of it, nor the cabeceiros who are in Ajuda. This was only arranged between the two and a few other people.

Ajuda having once been the first Portuguese commercial port, I asked that Your Majesty come to an understanding with the French, English and Spanish nations to come and trade here as they did in the past. Juliao did not like my friendship with Your Majesty to continue. To say that it was my order that the protectorate was established is entirely false, because nothing has happened with my knowledge. I don't give my land to any nation, not even the value of a spoonful, but I want friends to come and trade here.

Juliao de Souza did things that are not done in any part of the world, and for that, God punished him for his wickedness. He went as far as poisoning his own people such as Domingos F. de Souza, Gratta F. de Souza, Sabina de Souza, Reminda de Souza and Janna de Souza. These poor people died of poisoning two years ago.

Juliao de Souza owed me the sum of 38,100 pesos for workers he had been asked to buy back by the Portuguese settlers and at the end he told me that the Portuguese had not paid him and that they were not a good nation. But learning the lies and knowing how he had used this money in business after having given a part to his son Germano de Souza for the same purposes, while studying, I saw that Juliao de Souza wanted to create enmity between Your Majesty and I, but that's never going to happen.

The world was made that way. The whites have their Kings and I am the King of Africans. It is good that Your Majesty is against white people coming to take over African lands. If Europeans continue this way, Africans will soon be able to make brandy, fabrics, gin, glass beads and other items that they will transport to where European women sell their wares.

It is better that each nation govern its lands, the Whites in theirs with their Kings and I, the King of Dahomey, with mine. The whites have taken the land from the negroes, but the negroes cannot do the same.

I thank Your Majesty for having sent an emissary to my kingdom to verify the validity of the protectorate that Juliao and Dr. Meyrelles did without having my orders.

Signed: by order of King GLÉLÉ

by Antonio F. de Souza, translator, and Candido J. Rodriguez

King Kondo GBÈHANZIN (1889-1894)

Ahokponou - Kondo - Chadakogoundo - Gbè hin azin bo ayi djre (Behanzin) - Amountchiongbedji

Emblems: Shark and Egg

Motto: Nature holds the mystical Egg which the Earth praises and proclaims. I am the King of sharks. I will not give up an inch of my kingdom. The shark is in the sea and waits for the boats to capsize. Invaders, be afraid of me!

Birth: 1845 or 1844 (Abomey, Benin)

Death: 1906 (Blida, French Algeria)

After his death, he was cremated and his ashes were interred in Algeria before being exhumed and transported to Dahomey decades later for a reburial.

Gbè hin Azin bo Ayi djrè

The popular translation "The world holds the egg that the earth desires." is wrong. Swiss Claude Savary's proposition "The world holds the egg that the earth measures." is an improvement on the previous one but it falls into the trap of word-for-word translation which is inappropriate here.

A sign positioned in front of the Behanzin palace in Djimè in Abomey, indicates: "the germ of all manifestation of the earth". This definition captures the depth and symbolism of the name, but it's a bit too short and contracted for anyone to understand.

"Gbè" means Life as in "Nature".

"hin" means "to hold"

'Azin" means "egg" and more precisely "the Cosmic Egg" that is to say "the germ of all manifestations of life on earth" "bo" with the "o" sounding like the word "word" or "for" is a conjunction that connects the two parts of the sentence and means "and" or "that"

"Ayi" means here "the Earth" or "the world », meaning all the living beings (humans, animals and plants) as detailed in the King's panegyric.

"Drjè" means here "to proclaim" and "to praise the merits of"

Nature holds the mystical Egg (the germ of all manifestations of life) and the Earth praises and proclaims it.

It is this Egg that is the object of praise and worship. Nature manifests itself spontaneously but there is an Active Principle which breathes life into it. This Active Principle in other civilizations is called Spirit. With Christians it is the Divine Breath. For Astrophysicists like Einstein and Tyson, it is Energy. For Behanzin, it's the Egg. And in his omnipotence (rightly or wrongly), he considered himself to be this Egg or his only representative on Earth at this precise moment (not just in Danxomè, but in the whole world, including on the seas and beyond).

Panegyric of Behanzin in Fongbe and in English

Axòsu Gbèxàzì
O King Gbèhanzin

Gbê wê hin azin bo ayi jrë
Nature holds the mystical Egg that the Earth proclaims

Atin e jò do ayi o ji le
The trees that grow on the earth

Hwi ai wê jrè
It's you they proclaim and praise

Kan e jò do ayi o ji le
The lianas that grow on this earth

Hwi ai wê jrë
It's you they proclaim and praise

Vodü e do ayi o ji le
All the vodun on this earth

Hwi ai wê jrè
It's you they proclaim and praise

Gbètò e jò do ayi o ji le
The humans on this earth

Hwi ai wè jrë
It's you they proclaim and praise

Gbè wê xe azï bo ayi jrê
Nature holds the mystical Egg that the Earth proclaims

Axòsu aja gidigidi
O thou valiant ruler Adja (Behanzin is of Adja descent and origins like all Fon people. Before Allada it was Adja Tado, and before Adja it was Nigeria, and so on, all the way to the birthplace of humanity.)

Gbohwele fo adàn bò agbeji non lo

When the shark gets angry, the ocean becomes unbearable and calms down. (When the shark gets angry, all other animals disappear and the ocean calms down: Gbogbowele dje adan hou min gble)

Hwi ai Sogwe gbatò
Ye who destroyed Sogwe

("Sogwe" was a town of the Ouatchi people. "Asogwe" is a stylized type of calabash, so the phrase can have another deeper mystical meaning.)

E ni axòsu di xa
Honor to the king

Këinglo, aman da ma glo hwèdo
The enemies will be punished like leaves being cut up

Axòsu aviti gbajagbaja
O king who is mighty like a great trap

Aviti gbajagbaja nò so lan do xumë
A powerful trap that catches prey in the ocean

Cacalua gbatò
He who defeated Cacalua (chief of the Nago)

Adawuli gbatò
He who defeated Adawuli (probably another chief of the Nago)

So je de bo' agön glo
Lightning falls on the ronier palm tree, but spares it.

(This is the motto of King Agôglo who was the jòtò or guardian ancestor of Gbèhanzin)

Gbêxazï bo ai jrè
Nature holds the mystical Egg that the Earth proclaims

Hwi ai Sogwe gbatò
Ye who destroyed Sogwe

Sogwe'xòsu Dega hutò
Ye who killed Degâ, king of Sogwe

Dokome, Dàngbo gbatò

Ye who destroyed Dokomé and Dangbo

(Two villages on the Ouémé river near Porto-Novo. Abomey's incursions into this region served as a pretext for France to start a war with Dahomey because these territories were allegedly covered by the protectorate of France on Porto-Novo.)

Këinglo, aman da ma glo hwêdo

The enemies, we will punish them by cutting them like leaves

Ekpë Agbo hutò

He who killed Ekpë Agbo (a young man who went around saying he was more powerful than a buffalo.)

B'agala dele

Example of courage

Dada Sonigala lo adëtô

The intrepid King Sonigala (symbolic name of King Gbèhanzin comparing him to a tall mountain)

Originally called Ahokponou, he became Kondo the shark before being popularly known as Gbèhanzin Aijrè, whom the French would transform into Béhanzin. He gave the French colonists more trouble than any other African resistance fighter, becoming the icon of an entire continent for generations.

Born in 1845 (or end of 1844), Kondo became in 1875 Vidaho (crown prince chosen by his father King Glèlè), and acceded to the throne towards the end of 1889. He was crowned King on January 6, 1890 under the strong name of Gbèhanzin Aïdjrè.

Gbèhanzin devoted the short duration of his reign (1889 to 1894) to strengthening the power of his army, and to developing commerce, architecture and the arts. "A country is only great if it is free, I will never give up a piece of the land of my ancestors," he said. The city of Cotonou was the main point of conflict between France and Danxomè. The situation deteriorated when France built a wharf in Cotonou in 1891 to facilitate the landings of its ships. Gbèhanzin refused to grant France the right of occupation and free use of the city of Cotonou, in violation of an earlier agreement with Glèlè. In response the French navy attacked Dahomey by bombarding the coast of Cotonou, a large part of the inhabitants was massacred. True to his ideal of negotiating first before fighting, King Gbèhanzin used all possible means to avoid war. In 1893 he even sent an official negotiating mission to Paris, France, which was ignored not only by President Sadi Carnot but by the entire French government. He also sent several letters. But all of these efforts did not prevent war.

The Danxome army was well organized and was built with courage and bravery. The king was always present on the ground alongside his troops and was a difficult strategist to overcome. When the fighting became too deadly for his army, he withdrew and adopted a strategy of resistance from the bush. Modern revolutionary armies will adopt similar guerrilla techniques in the twentieth century. He resisted for several months without ever being caught despite the considerable means and extreme methods deployed by the adversary. At the end, General Dodds used cunning and treason to get him out of the bush, promising to take him to the President in France.

During his time underground when he was evading the French troops, King Gbèhanzin's mother, whom he loved very much and who was already old, committed suicide (with incantatory words and/or by poisoning with a special drink) at the suggestion of her son, because she was tired of running in the bush with her son and feared that the French would humiliate and kill her if she returned to one of the palaces. It is better to die with dignity than to live with shame or opprobrium. Some (less reliable) versions suggest that he killed her himself, but this is implausible. Gbèhanzin's concern was to prevent her from being captured by the French, and to be able to give her an honorable funeral and all the rituals that would guarantee her rest and a glorious stay in the afterlife. He did this and buried his mother in the village which became Nontche-digbe (burying my mother) then Nontcherigbe and nowadays Atcherigbe.

Gbèhanzin left Abomey to join Cotonou on January 28, 1894. He embarked from Cotonou on February 11, 1894 and arrived in Martinique at Fort Tartenson on March 30, 1894. Gbèhanzin left Martinique in 1906 and died a few months later in Algeria, on December 10 1906. He was buried in the Saint-Eugène cemetery in Algiers. His remains (ashes) returned to Dahomey in 1928 (22 years later). Even after his death, he still scared the French occupiers.

Gbéhanzin's exile court included: 4 of his wives (Etiomi, Senoncon, Menousoue, Dononcoue), his 3 daughters (Mecougnon, Kpotassi, Agbopanou), his young son Ouanilo who was 7 years old, his secretary Adandedjan (a relative of his), an interpreter Pierre Fanon and Falegue (wife of Pierre).

Marie-Francois Sadi Carnot, the French president Behanzin wanted to meet before being exiled to Martinique, was born in 1837 and took power in 1887 in France aged 50. When Behanzin understood General Dodds's cunning and realized that he was not going to be led to the leader of the French, he cursed them and prophesied about them. Strangely or by mere coincidence, on June 24, 1894, a few months later, Sadi Carnot was assassinated by the Italian anarchist Caserio.

Far from his native land, on which the French flag already hung, Behanzin had symbolically defeated the "king" of the white invaders.

List of the children of GBEHANZIN

- OUANILO (WANILO) ARISTIDE ARINI
- KPOTASSI (NAN MITON)
- MECOUGNON
- AGBOKPANOU (ABOPANOU) NAN DOHOUETON
- AWAGBE
- NAN ADJAYIWO
- Other children

Gbèhanzin and his party in Martinique in 1895

Gbèhanzin and his party in Algeria in 1905

First Letter from Béhanzin to the President of the French Republic, April 17, 1890

In November 1889, Jean Bayol, representative of the French Republic, Governor of Porto-Novo, came from the capital of Dahomey to make a contract (a convention) concerning the question of Cutona (Cotonou) and when for the first time, we chatted together, the same Jean Bayol told me that the two contracts that were in the power of France had been recognized as tainted with deceit, and that even by the interpreters and that King Gilli (Glélé) was only asking that the unloading of goods and all things was allowed to take place there so that they could continue on their way to Porto-Novo, paying the old customs fees.

My father accepted and the same Jean Bayol left me a contract to this effect, and in the meantime my father found himself indisposed and the same Jean Bayol went to bed; and no longer being able to come to any contract and seeing that the problems continued to be great, I was forced to dismiss Jean Bayol who was very well received by my father. It was sent on December 28th and on the 30th of the same month my father Glélé died. I ascended to the throne on January 1, 1890, and Jean Bayol had a present of fabrics which my father gave him and for Your Excellency. And on February 17 of this year I received notice, by letter, that the French merchants of Ajuda had established themselves in the Cypriano Fabre house, breaking a large number of bottles containing drinks, bottles empty for fortification and having loaded weapons.

Having learned of this, I immediately sent my authorities who were with me in the capital, to find out. And the very day they arrived in Ajuda, namely, on February 21, Jean Bayol had Cutona (Cotonou) bombarded without giving me any notice, killing the small number of people who were there by setting it on fire, imprisoning the authorities and sending them to Porto-Novo to have them delivered to my enemy, King Toffa. In the act of the bombing, gunshots were exchanged on both sides; and on the 16th day a night war was waged and people were lost on both sides, without my having been informed. I am very surprised that

France, which is a very old friend of the Kings of Dahomey, and has been doing so for many years to this day, when there is no other trade in my ports than French trade, did such a thing without warning me. In the meantime, I captured eight Europeans and I will wait until Jean Bayol has freed my representatives, and even, in terms of mistreating them, although as traders they did not have had to get involved in politics and war affairs, since they are not soldiers, I will wait for Your Excellency to justify this way of acting by Jean Bayol towards me.

I received from the latter the presents that Your Excellency sent me in the name of the French government, only I regret that, being an ancient friend of France, no one sent me any feelings of condolence with regard to the loss of my father, since other European nations did. As the Ajuda traders behaved badly, I took them prisoner; I ordered the factories to be closed and I had the sheiks put their employees who are currently in the same houses, only the Arrikote, Godony and Abome caraiz fled to Cutona (Cotonou) before the said affair. I gave orders and placed guards so that nothing was stolen from the factories. Disputes with French officers are very numerous and have occurred over and over again and Your Excellency has yet to take any action in this regard.

May God preserve the days of Your Excellency for many years.
H.M. the King of Dahomey

German cannon used by the army of Gbèhanzin

Second Letter from Béhanzin to the President of the French Republic

Cana Goumé, April 30, 1890 2 a.m.

Mister President,

Our friendship for France has always been very strong and every day we give new proof by treating our best and showering with gifts the Europeans who are in our power. It was Mr. Jean Bayol who fought the Cotonou war, pushed by King Toffa; France is not our friend. Toffa is the King of Porto-Novo because of us. His people did not want to accept him and it was on our message that he ascended to the throne. Why does he declare himself our enemy without cause? He is very happy and satisfied with the death of our father and on this occasion urged Mr. Bayol to wage war on us.

Oueffin wanted to make war on Toffa. We beat this country and all the prisoners of Porto-Novo that we met, we returned them to Toffa and yet he was unhappy with this war, giving false pretexts and lies that we did not give him back all his people. Now why start this Cotonou war for no reason whatsoever? Mr. Bayol called our authorities at the factory, locked them up and afterwards launched his soldiers to massacre all the people: the small children, the pregnant women were also massacred and we were not warned of this war. In Dahomey we have treated Mr. Bayol as the representative of France; we showered him with gifts and loaded him with gifts for yourself, Mr. President. We do not yet know if we sent them to you.

Our desire is that you would be kind enough to send an officer from your household to us to deal with matters of litigation.

As for Cotonou, my father never gave it and we will never give in. This is impossible for us, because if we do it would be a serious prejudice for us and the thunder would crush anyone who wanted to stay in this territory.

In eight days at the latest, the hostages will be in Whydah and the French authorities will have to hand over our prisoners to Cotonou under the same conditions as they were before, otherwise our troops will continue to destroy all the oil palms in the territory of Porto-Novo. . We have already sent our troops to destroy these palm trees to punish Toffa and the French soldiers have advanced against our troops. Why ? We are not waging war on France. It's at the King of Porto-Novo.

BÉHANZIN AHI - JÉRÉ King

Made at the Palais of Cana Goumé

Letter from Béhanzin to Admiral de Cuverville

Abomey Palace, August 18, 1890, 4 p.m.

Mr. Admiral,

Her Majesty says that she is quiet here without harming anyone and that it is the Europeans who have come to disturb the peace of her kingdom.

She says that God in principle created the Black and the White, each to inhabit the land that has been designated to him. White is in the business of trade and black must do business with white, that blacks do no harm to whites, and likewise whites should not harm blacks.

When two people are friends and one meets one that divides them, you should not send such a person here. And yet this is what Mr. Jean Bayol did. So in France there are very good people, the same in Dahomey and it was enough to Mr. Jean Bayol to lose everything.

The Kings of Dahomey from the beginning of their kingdom never gave their territory, they cannot, it is impossible. Europeans can stay in Cotonou if they need to, in return for an allowance each year. He says that just as the Fathers work for God and find the word of God, so the Kings of Dahomey work for their land and cannot leave it.

France will pay the King per year: in gold 1,500 (one thousand five hundred) pounds sterling or 7,500 piastres in silver (seven thousand five hundred silver piastres). This is the account the King receives every year from the decimers.

It was Toffa who started the intrigues. Since the French do not want His Majesty to wage war on him, please take care that Toffa remains quiet and does not seek any more quarrels. So the King of Dahomey will not attack him, especially now that the King of Dahomey is France's friend, because that would be a shame for him.

Regarding the city of Ouémé, the King of Dahomey will never stop the war because since ancient times the King of Ouémé has always waged war in Dahomey, since the time of King Accaba.

The King of Ouémé who brought war to Dahomey is called Iaazi. He burned down the King's own house and the King of Dahomey killed him. This town of Ouémé is near Dahomey and is not in the territory of Porto-Novo.

When the King of Dahomey died, Toffa did not send any gifts for the funeral. Toffa then sent a man called Padonou and the King gave him many presents for Toffa; the other Kings of Porto-Novo always sent presents when a King dies in Dahomey and this thing Toffa did is very wrong. When the Kings of Porto-Novo die, the Kings of Dahomey still send gifts for the funeral.

In Whydah, Godomey, Abomey-Calavi, Avrékété, the whites can trade as before. In the factories of Whydah, the King put a person to guard them, as well as Avrékété, Godomey, Abomey-Calavi. When the French bombed Whydah, then the inhabitants and guardians of the factories of Godomey returned to Whydah to wage war.

The people of Ouémé, then (...) came to Godomey-ville and Godomey-plage and stole everything that was in the factories. When Whydah's soldiers heard about it, they sent people to catch the thieves, but the thieves fled and the soldiers could only grab two people whose heads they cut off. The heads are in Godomey.

Everything that was in Cotonou, cowries, guns, powder etc ... was taken, as His Majesty heard it said. All the good books, papers about the decimers, have been burned.

His Majesty absolutely does not want soldiers to come to live in the French Fort. It was only because of Mr. J. Bayol that the French were taken. His Majesty in order to avoid any misunderstanding and intrigue will have the soldiers withdrawn from the Portuguese Fort by his cabéceres also my arrival in Whydah. So, she said, the French government sees that there is no need to put troops in the French Fort.

All white people will be treated well and nothing will ever happen to them. And if the King allows the French to land then it is the King who has lost the confidence of the French and the people will say that the King treats the whites well, it is because of the soldiers and not because of the friendship that has always existed between France and Dahomey.

The French will make a contract that they will never wage war on Dahomey and the Dahomeans will do the same and so the Dahomeans will never kill a Frenchman. In this way the two peoples will be eternally friends.

The King of Dahomey Signed: BÉHANZIN AHI - DJÉRÉ

Written by me at the King's own dictation and in his own words and style.

Signed: A. Dorgère Catholic missionary, chaplain of the expeditionary corps on a special mission in Dahomey

First Letter of Béhanzin to Ballot

Dahomey, March 29, 1892

To Monsieur Ballot, Governor of Porto-Novo,

I am sending you these two lines to know the news of your health and at the same time to tell you that I am very astonished by the recade that Bernardin brought to the cabécère Zohoncon for communicating to me about the six villages that I destroyed there three or four days ago.

I guarantee you are very wrong. Have I been to France a few times to wage war against you? Me, I stay in my country, and whenever an African nation hurts me, am I not going to punish it? It doesn't concern you at all. You were very wrong to send me this recade, it is a mockery; but I don't want to be laughed at, I repeat that I don't like that at all. The recade you sent me is a joke and I find it extraordinary. I'm still standing up for you and don't want to have these stories.

If you're not happy with what I'm telling you, you just have to do whatever you want, and I'm ready to go. You can come with your troops or you can go ashore to wage a bitter war against me. Nothing else.

Accept, Mr. Governor, my sincere greetings.

BÉHANZIN, King of Dahomey

Statue of Gbèhanzin in Goho (Abomey, Bénin)

Second Letter of Béhanzin to Ballot

Dahomey, April 19, 1892

I have just been informed that the French Government has declared war on Dahomey and that the matter has been decided by the chamber of France.

I warn you that you can start on any points you want and that I myself will do the same. But I advise you that if one of my villages is hit by the fire of your cannons, such as Kotonou, Godomey, Abomey-Calavi, Avrékété, Whydah and Agony, I will march directly to break Porto-Novo and all the villages belonging to the King from Porto-Novo.

As for what happened in the Ouémé river, you are the one involved, because when the Dahomeans are in the countryside, no one should be able to see or disturb them. If you hadn't come to war against me on the way to Atchupa, I wouldn't have done anything to you first. When a stranger comes to my house, let me know, and since you came to my house with a steamer, my troops thought you were coming to wage war on them again. That's why they started firing gunshots at the steamer.

About the Ouémé river, I told you several times and warned you by letters that you should not go there because I always had troops on this side and this is where the Dahomeans go to go and fight their enemies. I have told you several times that this river belongs to me and not to Porto-Novo or to anyone other than me.

Now I am coming to tell you, if you remain quiet, I too will remain quiet and we will remain in peace. If for example you do something, I will ruin everything in general and trade as well, and trade with other nations.

The first time I didn't know how to war, but now I know. If you start the war, I have troops ready for it. I have so many men they look like Worms coming out of the holes. I am the King of the Blacks and the Whites have nothing to do with what I do. The villages you tell me about are mine, they belong to me and wanted to be independent, so I sent them to destroy them and you always come to complain.

I want to know how many independent French villages have been broken up by me, King of Dahomey. Please be quiet, do your business in Porto-Novo, so we will always remain in peace as before. If you want war, I'm ready. I will not finish it anyway it would last a hundred years and kill me 20,000 men.

No one will ever know anything that I have just written to you. I'm waiting for your answer, but if France wants to go to war on me, I don't want you to warn me, because I am always ready on all points.

I am informed of everything, I know the number of millions that France wants to spend to start the war again. I am very knowledgeable. I received the letter you sent me by Zonahocon from Cotonou to Whydah, as well as the one you confided in the leader of the Dekanmè. I received them both and took note.

BEHANZIN

Letter from the Ouidah authorities to Mr. Ballot

Ouidah, March 30, 1892

To Monsieur Ballot, Governor of Porto-Novo,

The message that you conveyed to the chief of Cotonou was received by us, chiefs of Whydah, belonging to H.M. King Béhanzin of Dahomey. There is little we can tell you now about your post.

Admiral Cavelier de Cuverville sent Father Dorgère to H.M. the King of Dahomey to settle matters during the blockade. The King of Dahomey ordered Father Dorgère to write to the Admiral, and he responded on August 18, 1890. We have this letter. It is written in this letter that Dahomey will never stop fighting against the country of Ouémé; the reason is that, in the days of the old Kings, Ouémé waged a war against Dahomey! It was in the time of King Akaban! The King of Ouémé who fought this war was called Yazahé. It was he who burned down and completely destroyed the King's palace in Abomey. The Ouémé I am talking about has never been part of your kingdom and does not belong to Porto-Novo, but is indeed in Dahomey. If the admiral has never shown you this letter, you can send a messenger to Ouidah to take a copy.

Now we say to you, we the leaders, about the message that you sent to the King by the chief Zohoncon, that if the French intend to make the war in Dahomey, you will be cause that Porto-Novo will be destroyed as well. than all the cities of the interior. We let you know once again that Porto-Novo, not being in the sea but on land, is at the King of Dahomey; for everything on earth belongs to the King of Dahomey. What we can advise you, we, the chiefs of Ouidah, is to go up to see H.M the King Béhanzin of Dahomey, yourself if you want to arrange your business.

YOVOGAN, COUSSOUGAN and the leaders of the Agora.

The Army of Gbèhanzin (Illustration, L'Intransigeant, 1902)

First Letter from Général Dodds to Béhanzin

Porto-Novo, June 2, 1892

Appointed by the President of the Republic to the higher command of the French establishments located on the Slave Coast, I arrived in Cotonou on May 28. My astonishment was great to learn on disembarking that, in defiance of the rights of nations, you were illegally detaining three French traders in Ouidah and that you had again violated the commitments freely made by your representatives on October 3, 1890, by invading the territory of French protectorate that your troops still occupy today in Cotonou, Zogbo and Décamé.

I believe I should remind you of the terms of article 1 of the arrangement of October 3, 1890: "The King of Dahomey undertakes to respect the protectorate of the kingdom of Porto-Novo and to refrain from any incursion into the territories. being part of these protectorates. It recognizes the right of France to occupy the territory of Cotonou indefinitely."

As a consequence of the stipulations of the aforementioned convention, I beg you in your interest:

1° To release and return either to Cotonou or to Grand-Popo, the three French people currently detained in Ouidah.

2° To withdraw from Cotonou, Zogbo and the shores of the left bank of the Ouémé, from Dogba, the posts and detachments there.

I hope you will uphold my just demands as soon as possible.

Hello.

DODDS

Letter from General Dodds to the Authorities of Ouidah

I received your letter of June 14 addressed to Mr. Ballot in Porto-Novo and which was probably intended for me.

I am surprised at how confidently you say that the King of Dahomey is the friend of all Europeans.

You have to believe that in your thinking there is an exception for French people, because I would not otherwise explain to myself the attitude of King Béhanzin for several months; I am surprised that he has not yet responded to the letter I wrote to him informing him of my arrival in Benin as a representative of the French Government.

I see no reason to stop denying access to our possessions to the Dahomeans when they opened the gunner hostilities mounted by the lieutenant governor and the commander of the troops; when they still continue to support princes of Porto-Novo who are enemies of France, and especially when they maintain warriors in the territories dependent on our protectorate.

Hello.

A. DODDS

Second Letter from Général Dodds to King Béhanzin

June 20, 1892

Your letter of June 10 reached me in Porto-Novo on the 18th of the instant. You were kind enough to send it to me in response to my letter of the 2nd of the same month in which I invited you in the most conscious way:

1° To release the three French people illegally detained by your order in Ouidah.

2° To withdraw from Cotonou, Kobbo and the villages on the left bank of the Ouémé, from Dogla to Dogba, the posts and detachments of your army which are still there today.

Thank you for immediately granting my first desideratum, but allow me to marvel at the strange, childish and even ironic response you felt you should make to my second request.

The arrangement of October 3, 1890, the commitments of which you assure you have always scrupulously observed, stipulates "that treaties or conventions previously concluded between France and Dahomey remain intact". However, the convention of April 19, 1878 concedes in full ownership to the French Government a territory of six kilometers of coast on which are the villages of Cotonou and Zogbo. You will therefore allow me, in consequence, to regard as not very serious your claims on these two French villages.

On the other hand, we are entitled not to attach more importance to your alleged property rights over the province of Bas-Ouémé because the last of your subjects knows very well that the limit of your possessions on the side of the east is the river of So or Zounou to the lagoon of Tjibé-Akpomé and the lagoon of Ouovimé to Dogba.

Quinto, Zougomé, Dankoli, Ahenta, Denko, Biko, Agloloué, Agongué, Dawémé and Kétin-Sota that you looted and burned down last March are indeed on French territory and your troops could not ignore it since they have removed, lacerated and destroyed the French flags that these villages of King Toffa displayed.

The same is true of the left bank of the Ouémé, from Dogla to Dogba, which your soldiers still illegally occupy today; Isn't the leader of Dékame whom you pushed into rebellion and whom you still support a rebellious subject of the King of Porto-Novo?

I will not insist more on the importance that must be attached to your statements nor on the value of the feelings you say you have towards the French, feelings that are not in agreement, you will admit

1 ° With the unspeakable attack which Lieutenant-Governor Ballot and the commander of the troops were subjected to while sailing peacefully in a French gunboat in waters undisputedly belonging to France;

2 ° With the previous letters that you or your leaders sent, from March 19 to May 1, to the representative of the Republic in Porto-Novo.

Be that as it may, and despite the little credit that should be given to your claims, I felt it my duty to forward them to my Government which will assess them and inform me of its decision in their regard, a decision that will be happy to communicate with you as soon as it reaches me. In the meantime, not only do I maintain the formal prohibition made to the Dahomeans to circulate on the roads and lagoons of Porto-Novo, but also I inform you that this measure is completed by the prohibition of all communication with the ports of Dahomey, the French government having decided and notified the foreign powers that from the 18th of this month the blockade would be established on the coasts of our possessions in the Gulf of Benin.

Hello.

A. DODDS

Voluntary surrender of Gbèhanzin to Dodds (Illustration)

Declaration of forfeiture and banishment of King Béhanzin

Porto-Novo, December 3, 1892

On behalf of the French Republic,

We, Brigadier General Commander of the French Establishments, Commander of the Legion of Honor

By virtue of the powers conferred on us, Declare:

King Béhanzin Ahy - Djéré is deposed from the throne of Dahomey and banished forever from this country.

The kingdom of Dahomey is and remains under the exclusive protectorate of France and with the exception of the territories of Ouidah, Savi, Avrékété, Godomey and Abomey-Calavi which constituted the former kingdoms of Adjuda and Jacquin, which are annexed to the possessions of the French Republic.

The boundaries of the annexed territories are: to the West, the Ahémé river; to the north and east, the Savi River and the territory of Abomey-Calavi; to the south, the Atlantic Ocean.

A.DODDS

Third Letter from Béhanzin to the President of the French Republic

Fort-de-France, October 17, 1898

Mister President,

I come to present my sincere testimonies of the deep friendship I nurture for (Monsieur) the President of the French Republic, as well as to all his Ministers. For many years my ancestors have always been devoted allies of the French nation. The inhabitants of France were the first people who came to settle in the territory of Dahomey, which is why the word Zodjéagué in our language means the first foreigner or the Frenchman who arrives in our country.

Since my grandfather Guézo received Admiral Vallon in great friendship, the bonds of affection with the French Republic have continued to strengthen, although at that time I was still only a child. He received as gifts three magnificent flags whose lamp was surmounted by an eagle, the King of the birds as well as a host of sumptuous presents, and these French flags which still exist have always been waved at the head of the processions on the days of major festivals. . This proves the long friendship that my ancestors kept for France and when my father Glélé ascended the throne trade was opened to French industry; which facilitated the long duration of his reign. He even wrote to the French officer who was in Porto-Novo to let him know that I was called to succeed him. And when my name was Kondo, I saw a great number of French people whom my father always taught me to regard as great friends. Liars have misinterpreted the friendly relations between the two countries and declared war against my will, supported by Toffa the King of Porto-Novo, my personal enemy, as well as the enemy of Glélé my father. Despite all the misfortunes that Toffa is causing, I would never want to harm him, because he was a relative of mine, our blood is the same and God does not want revenge on his family. His war is a passing thing, but what will remain eternally is peace and friendship; wherever the French find themselves, the soil will remain respected in the same way for the inhabitants of Dahomey.

Messengers with explanations to avoid war were sent to Ouidah and Cotonou, but could only reach France by passing to my displeasure in the territory of Lagos.

I hope that France will understand the truth, my sincerity, for the friendship of a great people. Since leaving Dahomey, foreign climates have strained my health. My feelings must not remain unknown and after a long absence it would be sweet for me to maintain an eternal friendship with the French Nation on the very soil of Dahomey. My relations would henceforth be direct with the French by avoiding false interpreters and finally, I look forward to rendering my father the funeral honors which are due to the Kings of my country. If necessary, I will go to France myself to give the President of the Republic all the explanations with frankness and friendship. I lavish my affectionate feelings on Your Excellency and all the Ministers and in Dahomey my grand-nephews will always ignore the bad days of the war.

BÉHANZIN - AÏJÉLÉ

Letter from Béhanzin to Congressman Gerville Reache

Fort-de-France, October 10, 1902

Mr. Congressman,

Allow Béhanzin to recommend himself to the influence of the generous Member of Parliament for Guadeloupe. He knows how eager you are to help just causes, and he is confident that his will find support in you. I have been in Martinique for 8 and a half years, victim of the intrigues of Toffa, King of Porto-Novo, and the perfidy of the performers, bought by him, who deceived both the French, my friends and me. In this long period, all your compatriots of the sister Colony, all the highest military and civilian officials, like the most humble Martinique, can attest that I have always shown the greatest love and the greatest interest for France and the republican solemnities, at the same time as the most cordial friendship for the French.

I lost in the horrible catastrophes which destroyed St-Pierre and the villages of the North, a great number of sincere friends, big and small, I shared your immense pain, in the loss of your darling son, the pain too of France, in front of the partial ruin of its beautiful colony. But these phenomena, unknown to me and appalling, complete the destruction of my health, already shaken by exile.

Indeed, Mr. Congressman, you are aware that when, on my own initiative, I went to Colonel Dodds, I spontaneously asked him to take me to France, to confer with the Head of State and clarify the misunderstanding I was the victim of.

So I thought I was going to France, while I was headed to Martinique. You will easily understand my anguish and my sadness, for eight years that I have waited in exile for my justification; and I believe that if it could not be

yet it is for lack of information; I believe that if the Government were enlightened, I would already be restored to my old powers at the same time as in the friendship of France.

This is why, I decided to write on this subject, to the President of the Republic, and to the Minister of Colonies and to various colonial authorities, I hope that genuinely informed on the events of Dahomey, they will not delay. to bring back to his country an exile of eight years who was and still remains a great friend of France.

And I am counting on you, and also on your powerful friends, to support my cause with them, Mr. Deputy; on you, who can know us better, who know that the intrigues of the past that I could hardly overcome, will no longer be able to present themselves, since I will have by my side my son, educated by France, enlightened by his civilization, and who will be an effective intermediary between the French authorities and me.

I am, Mr Deputy, I repeat, a great friend of France, and I urge you to believe, at the same time as in my anticipated gratitude, in my feelings of affection for her, as for all her representatives.

BEHANZIN

First Letter from Béhanzin to the Governor of Dahomey

Fort-de-France, February 28, 1903

Mr. Governor,

It is with complete confidence in the humanity and the high spirit of justice of the representative of France in Dahomey that Béhanzin salutes you. The Kings of Dahomey have always been friends of France and France has always been friendly towards them. I was also very fond of the great nation, and the disagreements so unhappy, so regrettable which arose in our relations, are due only to the perfidy of the interpreters of Toffa, King of Porto-Novo, who at the same time deceived the French and me.

A victim of the criminal acts of these bribed agents, I have been in Martinique for ten years, in exile. During my long stay here, I was the object of great sympathy from the brave officers of the French army, from all the high officials of the country - those whom we found on our arrival as those who succeeded them - I was able to appreciate the qualities of French people, young and old; my love for them could only increase from this contact. But, Mr. Governor, despite everything, the exile is painful for the victims of the Dahomey expedition. Our common health is declining. The latest volcanic phenomena, so terrible and new to us, are destroying our health.

So, Mr. Governor, we are counting on your spirit of humanity to see our country again. I will be there for France, for French politics, a devoted agent and a faithful friend, a propagator of his ideas. Because, and despite all the setbacks, all my misfortunes which come from the fact that the French have been deceived, I remain a friend of your country.

So do not be afraid to shoulder a heavy responsibility, surrendering to my kingdoms. The gratitude alone that I owe you, if my esteem for France and the feeling of her power did not already distance me from it, would prevent me from becoming hostile to French power.

You can therefore, on this occasion, place your trust in me, Mr. Governor. It would be given to you, by intervening in my favor,

to make the French colonial power deeper in Africa, to obtain a friend and a collaborator. Thanks especially to the generous instruction given by France to my son Ouanilô, I could have been of effective assistance to you.

Allow me, Governor of Dahomey, to count entirely on your generous intervention, to give France one of the most reliable supports for its policy in Africa.

BEHANZIN

Second Letter from Béhanzin to the Governor of Dahomey

Fort-de-France, le 10 août 1903

Monsieur le Gouverneur,

J'ai l'honneur de venir une fois encore, réclamer l'appui de votre haute influence auprès de Monsieur le Ministre des Colonies.
J'ai tout récemment fait un dernier appel à sa bienveillance et à sa générosité, et je compte sur vous pour que cet appel réussisse.

Comme je l'ai dit à Monsieur le Ministre des Colonies, je suis resté un ami de la France : j'ai tout oublié du passé : et j'ai conjuré ce haut magistrat de repousser aussi les pénibles souvenirs de la guerre.
N'ayez aucune appréhension, aucune crainte des responsabilités que vous encourez en provoquant mon retour au Dahomey. Vous trouverez en moi un ami reconnaissant, et loin de regretter cet acte, vous ne pourrez que vous en féliciter.

Veuillez agréer, Monsieur le Gouverneur, l'assurance de ma vive sympathie et de ma reconnaissance anticipée.

BÉHANZIN
J'ai l'honneur de saluer, Monsieur le Gouverneur du Dahomey.

The letters are interesting and valuable.

We see at the start, when he was still in Abomey, a combative and threatening Behanzin who claims his rights with intransigence. There is a time to flex your muscles, and there is a time to pretend to be weaker than you really are so that you can surprise the opponent. In the case of Behanzin, we know that for the Second Franco-Dahomean War, the French were careful to apprehend and prevent the additional deliveries of British and German arms on which Behanzin was strategically relying.

The French themselves came with much greater military power than during the first campaign. In addition to French military officers, they had a large contingent of Senegalese soldiers requisitioned in the colony, Nago soldiers experienced in the war against Dahomean troops and soldiers from Toffa (the King of Porto-Novo) who knew the terrain of Southern Dahomey very well.

In the melancholy of Martinique, the King's tone changes and he now positions himself as a friend of France, ready and able to help them if they have the courage to return him to his native land.

Towards the end, he was sent to Algeria where he died, certainly on his native African land as he wished, but far from the Dahomean plains where he grew up.

Authentic photo of amazones (1894)

Photo of King Agoli-Agbo

DAHOMEY — Le dernier roi du Dahomey
Agoli-Agbo, frère de Behanzin

King Goutchili AGOLI AGBO
(1894-1900) et (1900-1940)

Emblem: foot stumbling against a rock, broom, bow

Motto: Beware! The dynasty of the Kings of Danxome stumbled, but it did not fall. The King is like a broom that pushes back his enemies.

Panegyric of Agoli Agbo in Fongbe and in English

Axosu Agoli Agbo
O King Agoli Agbo

Alada klë afò ma j'ai
Allada stumbles but doesn't fall to the ground

(After Gbèhanzîn's defeat, the French had his brother Goutchili appointed in his place. The new King took the name of Agoli Agbo (Beware of your way Abomey!) To assert that he had saved Dahomey from ruin. Allada. is the place of origin of the Abomean dynasty. Agbo = Agbome = Abomey)

Kle Agbo, klë Agbo sòwali
Abomey stumbles, Abomey stumbles and might fall

Axòsu to se gbe
O King that all listen to

Flase blo Alada to do e
The French reinstated the Allada kingdom

Lo bo Dàxomê se gbe
And Dahomey obeyed

Bo ni axòsu tòdida
Thou who call yourself King according to your father's will

(King Agoli Agbo, having been able to perform the ceremonies required for the solemn funeral of his father Glëlë, indeed deserved the throne of Dahomey.)

Togba na kpë vi bo tòdida
If the burden of the country is heavy for the child, his father will help him

Bo ni axòsu nugbo wèkê
Thou called the real King in front of the whole world

(The coronation of Agoli Agbo had been recognized by France and other European Nations.)

Bo Alada lo non sïmè
Allada now has to accept

Zo de do Agolïto
The land of Agonlin is burning

(To honor a deceased King, the Dahomean custom was that some slaves or captives were sacrificed to him. Agoli Agbo had to comply and launched troops against the village of Agonlin populated by Mahi who had laughed at the defeat of the Dahomey .This was one of the reasons used by the French to abolish the Dahomey royalty and to exile Agoli Agbo.)

Axòsu fë ma no vo
O King, hard to remove like a nail

Alada'xòsu fé ma no vo
O King of Allada, hard to remove like a nail

Fe ma nö vo nu alò
Hard to remove like a nail

(Another strong name of the king has the same meaning: "Jau xë nu alò ma i", what the hand grips does not escape. Allusion to the king's grip on power.)

Bo ni axòsu n'ò vivi
The king who sweeten things

Adokpo xè gbo degedege gbÔ nu ò vivi
Adokpö wisely holds the orange so it can ripen. (The orange symbolizes the kingdom.)

Axòsuvi, we de weto
O Prince, to each his gift

(That is, each King uses different methods to achieve his ends. Response to criticism from descendants of Gbëhànzïn.)

AdokpÔ vi zë, mò zë bo nò mia
The orange of Adopkpô's son, Why couldn't this orange ripen?

(After having known ruin and defeat, Dahomey may still find peace and prosperity under colonial rule.)

Akpakogan nla jo
The iron of the trap does not let go of its prey

Akà bi na futü do axito
The rope will snap in the market

(The King will stretch ropes in the marketplace to punish anyone who slander him.)

Tòsisa mò nò go tò kple te
The water streams come together

Ye to le kple sa kaka lo Kpëgla agbetò
After their long journey, they gather in the ocean of Kpëgla

(Agoli Aqbo had King Kpëgla for jòtò or guardian ancestor. Kpëgla previously used this metaphor after his victory over the xwëda chief Agbamu.)

Hwi wê ye co ko na we
They can only come to you

Bò ni axòsu glë zÔ Yovo
Thou the King who led the Europeans to the fields

Gle zo Yovo.bò xomènÒhu agbetò
The ocean rejoiced when the Europeans were led to the fields

Xwêda axòsu Agbamu hutò
He who killed Agbamu, King of Xwêda

(feat accomplished by Kpengla, jòtò of Agoli Agbo)

N'xòmla we lade
We praise you, Ô King

Axòsu Agoli Agbo
O King Agoli Agbo

Zo de do Agôlïto
The land of Agonlin is burning

Vèhûdo hutò
He who killed Vèhûdo

Adamaxo hutò
He who killed Adamaxo

Janâsu hutò

He who killed Janâsu

(Vèhûdo, Adamaxo, and Janâsu were all chiefs of the Agonlin people)

B'agala dele

Example of courage

Lade to xo do zogonutò lo adetò

O intrepid King, who conquered the country with guns

(The Dahomeans had known about firearms for a long time, but they only had old muskets or flintlock guns, apart from a few cannons bought from the Portuguese and the Dutch merchants. Already during the war against the French, King Gbehànzin succeeded in obtaining rapid-fire weapons, including a French-made machine gun that can still be seen on display at the Abomey Historical Museum.)

Brother of Behanzin and chief of the military staff during his reign, GOUTCHILI (who was called HLO DJEVIVI at his birth in 1839) was installed on the throne on January 29, 1894 under the strong name of AGOLI AGBO, by the French in replacement of his brother forced to exile in Martinique. The French interference and blessing reinforced the rumors of betrayals that wrongly weighed on this king.

Agoli Agbo is accused of being involved both in the fall of Abomey, but also in the dismantling of Gbèhanzin's secret dens, resulting in the annihilation of his spiritual strength; and sealing the doors to the possibility of any return without the approval of the French government. Such return would have threatened the reign of the new King Agoli Agbo and the colonial administration the French were installing. These rumors have long been a source of misunderstanding and division between the descendants of Agoli Agbo, the descendants of Gbèhanzin and members of the other royal families. We will never know all the twists and turns of the facts. However, it is worth pointing out that while Gbèhanzin regularly indexed King Toffa of Porto-Novo for his betrayals, he never reproached anything to his brother Agoli Agbo in his letters.

Therefore, and considering that Agoli Agbo was not even the first choice of the French for the succession, as well as the events which will follow, including his own exile, I personally believe in the innocence of Agoli Agbo. Gbèhanzin was certainly betrayed, but by someone else.

The French who expected Agoli Agbo to be a puppet king that they could manipulate at will, like they already installed in their other colonies, were very quickly disappointed and had to deport the new King. They then decided to dissolve the royalty of Danxomè altogether. Agoli Agbo was therefore exiled like his brother Gbèhanzin. From 1900 to 1910, he was detained in the city of Libreville in Gabon then in the town of N'DJOLE in Gabon, where he was locked in the same prison as SAMORY TOURE.

The grievances of the King, and those of his brothers and sisters back in Dahomey, led the colonial administration to consent to his return to Dahomey. However, the mistrust of the French remained great. He was placed under house arrest in Gblessogo on Adi's farm in the city of Savè for 15 years. In 1925, King Agoli Agbo was finally moved to Mougnon (Zou region). In 1927, the palace of Gbindo was completed and the King was at last able to return to Abomey (Zou).

A notable achievement to Agoli Agbo's credit is that he succeeded against all odds in performing all the statutory ceremonies for his father Glèlè. For this he did not hesitate to wage war on Agonlin, which enabled him to capture the slaves he needed for the required sacrifices. He was the last King in Dahomey to perform human sacrifices.

It was also Agoli Agbo who presided over the burial festivities of the remains of Gbèhanzin when they were finally returned from Algeria on March 9, 1928.

Agoli Agbo contributed a lot to the kingdom in the areas of culture, historic heritage and religion. We can list :

- the restoration of the temples of "ZOMANDONOU";

- the renovation of all the "DJEXO" of the Kings;

- the rediscovery of the burial places of Kings AGONGLO, GHEZO and GLELE and the celebration of the royal worships and rites due to them.

From an artistic standpoint, Agoli Agbo improved the rhythms AGBADJA, HOUNGAN and ATCHA. He specially created the GOKOUE rhythm on the occasion of the funeral celebration of his father King GLELE. He is the author of a multitude of historical songs.

Le King Agoli Agbo en 1894, Archives Getty

List of the children of AGOLI AGBO

- King TOGNI AHOSSOU WOUGOTON GANSE
- King AHLIHA AIDODODO
- DAH GBENON
- NAN WOUDIDI
- TOHOU
- FOUTOUDJEHOUNGBE
- AGBANI GASTON
- Other children

Geographic location of the private royal palaces in Abomey

King TEGBESSOU created the ADANDOKPODJI DAHO neighborhood in Abomey by installing a palace there.

King KPENGLA created the ADANDOKPODJI KPÈVI district by installing a palace there.

King AGONGLO created the ADAME district in GOHO and later the HUEGBO district in DJEGBE by installing a palace in each of those two locations.

King GUEZO created the GBECON/HOUNLI district by installing a palace there.

King Glèlè created the COVEKPA district in DJEGBE by installing a palace there.

King Gbèhanzin's palace is in the DJIME district.

King AGOLI AGBO's palace is in the GBINDO district.

The palace of Queen ZOGNIDI wife of GUEZO is in the SEDESSA district.

List of the KPODJITO, the mothers of the Rulers of Danxomè

Often ignored or overlooked, both by the historians of the Kingdom and by modern scholars, these women were the cornerstones of Danxomè and played a critical role in the palaces. I decided to include here this list that I previously published on Twitter to massive applause and appreciation from the culture-thirsty crowd in Benin.

Mother of King Houegbadja: Nan ADROU

Mother of King Akaba: Nan ADONON

Mother of reine Hangbé: Nan ADONON

Mother of King Agadja: Nan ADONON

Mother of King Tegbessou: Nan HOUANDJILE

Mother of King Kpengla: Nan TCHAYI (CAI)

Mother of King Agonglo: Nan SENOUME

Mother of King Guézo: Nan AGONTIME

Mother of King Glèlè: Nan ZOGNIDI

Mother of King Gbèhanzin: Nan ZEVOTIN

Mother of King Agoli Agbo: Nan KANAYI (KANNEYI AGONNOUTON)

Nan Zognidi: Wife, Mother and Grand-Mother of Kings

Nan Zognidi was the primary wife of King Guézo, mother of King Glèlè and grandmother of Kings Behanzin and Agoli-Agbo. She had a remarkable life strewn with pitfalls and triumphs; and is one of my ancestors.

After a long vacancy, her throne was rehabilitated and the person chosen to occupy it presently is my direct aunt Tokpo Sidonie who was coronated with the strong reign name of Nan Zognidi Sokewun. This section is about the original queen herself, not my aunt the current ceremonial queen.

NANYE ZOGNIDI KPODJITO AGOYI SINDOLE (Four-times-great-grandmother of Dallys-Tom MEDALI) was born in 1776 (or 1774), in Adakplame, Plateau, Benin, to Zoki (her dad) of Gbaka (the town where he lived) and to Houmin Ainon adikounvi ajoxoue nou (her mom, who was originally from the town of Aguigadji that she left to join her husband).

Nanyé Zognidi was a queen mother. She died in 1856, aged about 80, in Abomey, Zou, Benin.

Nanyé Zognidi has been married twice. She first married Alavo brother of Guézo, before marrying King GUEZO Gakpé Agbahaida of Danxomè after the death of her first husband.

King GUEZO and Nanyé ZOGNIDI Kpodjito Agoyi Sindolé had five children:

- King Glèlè Badohoun Gbingni of Danxomè born in 1802
- Noudai Guézo
- Dako Guézo
- Nanni Nagni Guézo
- 5th Guézo child of unknown name who lived very briefly

The many names of the queen

stage 1 (childhood in Mahi / Nago country) -> **Agoyi** (her "false" twin has returned to the spirit world at birth)

stage 2 (youth and captivity in Abomey, and first marriage with prince Alavo) -> **Djeto** (pearl of the waters)

stage 3 (marriage with Guézo, exile in Cana and Ouidah, majestic reign) -> **Nan Zognidi Kpodjito** (mother of the leopard or the future king) / **Adetegoungoun** (powerful) / **Gancame Kassinto** (politically active and influent) / **Sindolé** (water is beneficial and important) / **Francesca** = Catholic baptismal name in Whydah before her marriage to Guézo /.

Nan zognidi = dje nan nan xo zognidi = the rare royal pearl has undergone the test of fire, so that its name can resonate in echo for generations.

The procession came from Adakplame (in the current city of Kétou, which I had the pleasure of visiting during the major commemorations for the enthronement of the current queen). The procession included young virgin girls, young mothers and children (boys and girls).

The members (mainly girls and women) of this historic contingent are the DJETO or rare pearls brought back to continue the effort to "beautify" the kingdom. Their many descendants on the Zou plateau in Benin are the DJETOVI, also called for simplicity, DJETO like their illustrious ancestors. Queen Zognidi, through her husband Guézo's accession to the throne and her own remarkable biography, is the heroine of these people and the godmother of the many communities of families that have been created.

The work of Toussaint C. Ahomagnon with the elders of the community has made it possible to identify 56 main families which constitute the people that we can call DJETOVI or DJETO. This list, although incomplete, is quite extensive.

List of the DJETOVI of Danxomè

TOKPO	AVOLONTO
ALAGBE	BAHOUNON
SINSIN	AGBONANGO
CADOU	AZINGODO
DESSOU	AZOMA
AHOHOKPA	AGBANLIKPE
GOHOUNGO	ABLIBA
AZON	TESSAGOU
TCHIBO	ATCHASSOU
MONNOU	KPLEDEHOU
TOUNOU	LOKONON
TOUDE	HOUNON
GUEDEGBE	GBELI
AGBOGLO	NAHOUE
ZOTONGNINOU	DJISSONON
GBEMETONOU	MISSANON
ALIMAGNIDOKPO	ADJEHOUNON
DOHOUNKPE	GNISSOU
KODJROVODOUN	HONDJENOU
TOKPONOU	AYIDOTE
NONNON	AGBOSSOUNON
ATIMBADA	AHOMANLANTO
AMOULO	HOUNDJO
HOUNLELOU	GNONGBE
LANGAN	FANDI
GBATLOSSI	TOGNANLIDE

AZOMAHOU	KANIEKO
AZONOUKPO	AGNANKANNON

Some of these families later split into many branches. We must also add the impressive and populous royal collectivity of Glèlè and descendants since Glèlè was the main fruit of the union between GUEZO and ZOGNIDI. Finally there are some people who are DJETOVI but who carry their paternal family name.

Ceremonial Kings of Abomey
(Kings of Danxomè after the French occupation)

AGOLI AGBO Goutchili (1900-1940) *[King in exile]*
SAGBADJOU Glèlè (1938-1982)
AIDODODO Ahliha Agoli Agbo (1940-1948) *[Schism]*
TOGNI AHOSSOU Agoli Agbo (1948-1983) *[Schism]*
 Throne is vacant (1983-1986) [Vacancy]
LANGANFIN Joseph (1986-1989)
DEDJALAGNI Agoli Agbo (1989-2018)
HOUEDOGNI Behanzin b.1943 (2000-2012) *[Schism]*
KEFA Sagbadjou (2018-present)

SAGBADJOU Glèlè (1938-1982)

He was just a ceremonial King, but he was still given a formal panegyric praise.

Panegyric of SAGBADJOU in Fongbe and in English

Axòsu xilili
O powerful King

Daxomè'xòsu xilili
Powerful King Dahomey

Xu wë jò xilili bo zu so
The sea mocks the mountain

Mo na ma kpiso gè
But the slander doesn't reach it

Mo na ma da do gè
Nobody can move you (because you are like a mountain)

Vi galagala ci wë do tò lo xwe
Courageous child who is comfortable in his father's house

(Sagbaju Glëlë resided in an annex of the royal palace.)

Bo ni axòsu axwàsi nukô
King similar to a colorful parrot

(axwàsi is also one of the stages of the Vodù initiation. We recognize the axwàsi by the parrot feather in their hair.)

Dâxomê axòsu axwàsi nukô
Dahomey King similar to a colorful parrot

So ma je kèsë do axwâsi nukô
Thunder never strikes the parrot. (At least the parrot species known as axwàsi according to the legend)

Xomêwêsïda bò logozo no go
The angry snake cannot harm the turtle hidden under a shell

Ani na do wa wè ka de ?
What could it do?

Bò ni axòsu adontü
King adontü (Hard to push around)

Johô ni ma fë ala nu adontü
Even the wind cannot lower the branches of the adontù tree

N'xom]ä we lade
I praise thou, ó King

N'xòmlà we asu e
I praise thou my dear

Caku caba agidi wolo
Cakucaba, the powerful charm (Cakucaba is. a symbolic name of King Agaja, who is the jòto of king Sagbaju Glëlë.)

Agìdi wolo, agidi wolo
powerful charm, very powerful charm

Dosu wè ni ago lo gù
Dosu pushes aside those who oppose him

(Dosu is another name of king Agaja)

Më xê" bo yi më nu la
He who attacks and snatches by force

Akwë d'asi we, avo d'asi we
You have plenty of money, and plenty of loincloths

Dosu lo biò de we a
Dosu does not ask for them

Vi d'asi we, asi d'asi we
You have plenty of children and wives

Axovi lo biò de we a
The prince (Dosu Agaja) does not ask for them

Ta e do kò towe nu le
It is the head on your neck

E biò we wê Kpòvèsa de
That Kpòvèsa is requesting

(Kpòvèsa, another name of Agaja which means furious panther. The panther kpò symbolizes the ancestor of the Fon people.

According to tradition, Agaja is the first to establish the human sacrifices in the annual rituals of the kingdom.)

A gbo ta towe so jo ni we
If you cut your head off and give it to him

Eneo a ka gbojè
Then you will be in peace

A ma ka gbo ta towe bo so jo ni we we
But if you refuse to give him your head

Ku Dosu lo do yi wè kaka lo
Dosu the death will follow you

E wa kpe we do fi de lo
Wherever you go

De tòvi de nu lo
Whether to the water or the fountain

Aikügbä gïgï de ji
Whether to a remote land

Sé flu de me
Whether in the middle of the grass

Kpòvèsa na so we zi do
Kpòvèsa will cut you down

Odaflo dagbedagbe ò e na gbidi
Your beautiful eyelids will be rubbed

Xwèda'xòsu Hufö hutò
By He who killed Huffon, King of the Xwèda people

Axwà jo su do nu Gbagidito
He who destroyed the army of the nation of Gbaguidi (Savalou)

N'xòmlà we lade
I praise thou, O King

N'xòmlà we as'wi e
I praise thou, O Master

Agoli Ago II Dedjalagni

Birth: 1931

Death: 2018 (87 ans)

I had the honor of meeting King Agoli Ago Dedjalagni twice: the first time as part of the symbolic ennoblement of my former Danish boss David Skov (Maersk Line Company), and the second time as part of the enthronement of the King of the Tokpo family. During each of these encounters I was filled with solemnity and he gave me an impression of great wisdom and calm. This may explain why he had the respect of both state authorities and the people, even beyond the limits of his kingdom. His nose cover or dust cover (which he inherited from Goutchili his ancestor and first Agoli Agbo) is certainly the distinctive sign that will remain in the collective memory of the Beninese. Before his accession to the throne, he worked as a policeman and retired.

On July 2, 2018, night fell on the kingdom. I was in America that day, but I was also affected by the news.

GBAGUIDI SOHA: Founder of the Savalou kingdom and Ancestor of the MEDALI family

Key takeaways:

Gbaguidi = Oba-Guidi = Powerful (Guidi) Chief (Oba)

Ahosu Soha = Ahosu Gbe So Ha Bo Ha Gni Do Gbe Min = King (Ahosu) refused to climb or ride a horse (Gbe So Ha) and (Bo) rode a wild buffalo in the woods (Ha Gni Do Gbe Min)

Agba Rakho ATOLOU, son of Dessou ATOLOU (his dad) and the princess daugher of king LIGBO (chief of the town of DAME, in the ZOU region) was born in 1557. He founded the kingdom of Savalou around 1600 and died in 1618.

So he could or should have been called "Gni-ha" since it was on a buffalo that he rode, and not on a horse "So-ha".

I received these explanations from the oral tradition but having recently come across an article written on this subject, I decided to include the article in full here and to add some corrections.

From a Wikipedia extract itself inspired by the writings of Emile Larose [Origines de Savalou et ses rois, 1928] and of Sylvain Anignikin [Histoire des populations Mahi, Cahiers d'études africaines, vol. 162, 2001]

Due to family inheritance disputes, or by accident during a night hunting party, according to other versions; or to punish the raiding of his néré tree (ahoua-tin), his only paternal heritage.

Dessou Atolou, an ethnic Houéda hunter, kills his brother and leaves his village of Mitogbodji near Sègbohouè, on the shores of Lake Ahémé in Mono (southwestern Benin) to settle in the village of Damè in Fon country. He falls in love with the daughter of Ligbo, the village chief, and marries her. From this union Agba Rhako was born.

Ligbo dies and it is decided that his successor will be the person who will succeed in taming and riding a wild buffalo.

It is unusual in Dahomey to determine royal succession by such a test. A ruler may choose to offer a princess in marriage by this method of selection. But royal succession is often determined in advance based on birthright. with a clear identification of the crown prince if they are many princes, or a potential regent when the crown prince is still a small child or unborn. Now when other princes or other people wish to challenge the crown prince, they usually do so with a mixture of violence and cunning.

According to another version, it was about choosing the best rider among the contenders for the throne. Rhako who was not necessarily the best horse rider, proposed that the competition be done with a buffalo instead of a horse, and was the only one to succeed. Rhako passes the test, becomes the village chief and is nicknamed So-ha.

An important element missing from this account is the reason why the new chief Rhako and his subjects suddenly left their Damè to move elsewhere. They settle in Houawé near Bohicon before later moving up the hills in Nago territory. By waging war against the locals, he ended up imposing his authority on these populations who then nicknamed him Oba-Guidi, which means true leader and great chief; nickname that will change to Gbaguidi over time.

During his time in Houawé, he maintains good neighborly relations with Do-Aklin, another chief in the region. After the latter's death, his sons Gangni-Hessou and then Dako-Donou succeed him and start disapproving the growing influence of Soha Oba-Guidi. Dako-Donou forcibly subdues all the chiefs in the Houawé region. Soha Gbaguidi to avoid the same fate, leaves once again and settles in the hills where he builds the city of Savalou. The version I received, puts the buffalo episode here and the taking of the name "So-ha".

Initially, Agba Rhako, Dako and Gangnihessou got along and were good friends. They frequently indulged in the game of "Adji" sometimes called "Awale" with other friends. This is why Agba Rhako did not receive at first the same deadly treatment as Adingni and the other Guédévi leaders.

It all started from a feud created by mutual friends who liked to compare the supposed or actual size of Dako's genitals and sexual abilities to those of his brothers and friends, especially Rhako who according to legend was very well endowed.

One day, in the grip of anger, Dako and his men ambushed Rhako in an assassination attempt. Trapped, Rhako (Soha) who was like his father a skilled hunter and knew powerful magical incantations; uttered a few words and a buffalo appeared from the bush. He climbed the buffalo and escaped, much to the bewilderment of Dako and his men.

This episode does not exclude the possibility that Rhako has already on one or more occasions in the past, rode a buffalo for exhibition or to save himself.)

Soha migrates north with his men, to settle in the region of Honhoungo, 80 kilometers north of Houawé, near the populous Nago Tchébélou village built on a hill. Soha Gbaguidi sets out to conquer this village and on the advice of a friend, uses a trick to reach his goal. He ties flaming straws to the legs of several pigeons which are sent to land on the roofs of the huts of Tchébélou which then burn to the ground. Soha offers the Yorouba chief of Tchébélou the help of his men to rebuild his village. The chief accepts and organizes a banquet of gratitude to kickstart the work of reconstruction.

Soha had weapons concealed in the raw materials allegedly destined to be used for the rebuild. After the inaugural banquet ended, at Soha's signal, his men took out their weapons and massacred the population of Tchébélou. The village emptied of its dead or fleeing inhabitants, Soha can easily settle with his men at the foot of the hill and founded the capital of his future kingdom which he baptized Sa-Avalou or Savalou (Sa: friendship and Avalou: homage) in homage to the friendship which made this conquest possible. Soha subdues the neighboring localities of Doïssa, Ouessè, Koutago, Zounzonkanmè and expand his territory.

This account is mostly correct and quite informative, apart from a few important details that I corrected along the way.

Royal Lists

Rulers of the Kingdom of Danxomè (1600-1900)

X - Various Patriarchs in Tado and Allada thru year 1600
1 - Chef Do Aklin (1600 - 1620)
2 - King (usurpateur) Dako Donou (1620-1645)
3 - King (honorifique) Gangnihessou (1620-1645)
4 - King Aho Houegbadja (1645-1685)
5 - King Houessou Akaba (1685-1708)
6 - Reine Tassi Hangbé (1708-1711)
7 - King Dossou Agadja (1711-1740)
8 - King Bossa Ahadé Tegbessou (1740-1774)
9 - King Kpengla (1774-1789)
10 - King Agonglo (1789-1797)
11 - King Adandozan Madogugu (1797-1818)
12 - King Ghézo (1818-1858)
13- King Glèlè Kinikini (1858-1889)
14 - King Kondo Gbèhanzin (1889-1894)
15 - King Agoli Agbo (1894-1940)
X - Various symbolic Kings (1940-present)

Rulers of the Kingdom of Allada

XIIe - XVe siècle: Various unknown chiefs

(c. 1400): LANDE ADJAHOUTO founded the kingdom

1400-1440: Lande Adjahouto

1440-1445: Aholuho Adja Adjahoutonon

1445-1458: De Noufion Adjahoutonon

1458-1470: Dassou Adjahoutonon

1470-1475: Dassa Adjahoutonon

1475-1490: Adjakpa Adjahoutonon

1490-1495: Yessou Adjahoutonon

1495-1498: Azoton Adjahoutonon

1498-1510: Yessou Adjahoutonon

1510-1520: Akonde Adjahoutonon

c.1520-1530: Amamou Adjahoutonon

c.1530-1540: Agagnon Adjahoutonon

c.1540-1550: Agbangba Adjahoutonon

c.1550-1560: Houeze Adjahoutonon

c.1560-1580: Agbande Adjahoutonon

c.1580-1585: Kinha Adjahoutonon

1585-1587: Mindji I Adjahoutonon

1587-1590: Akoli Adjahoutonon

1590: Kokpon founded the new kingdom

1590-1610: KOKPON DOGBAGRI Adjahoutonon

1610-1620: Medji II Hounoungoungou Adjahoutonon

1620-1660: Lamadje Kpokonou Adjahoutonon

1660-16XX: Tezifon Adjahoutonon

16XX-17XX: Gbagwe Adjahoutonon

17XX-1724 De Adjara Adjahoutonon

Mars 1724: Annexation of Allada by the kingdom of Danxomè after a military campaign led by King Agadja.

1724-1742: Direct rule by the Kingdom of Danxomè

1742: Two years after the death of Agadja, royalty is restored to Allada but the kingdom will be a vassal of the kingdom of Danxome until 1894 (year of conquest of Danxomè by France and deportation of Behanzin to Martinique).

1742-1792: Mijo Adjahoutonon

1792-1842: Ganhwa Adjahoutonon

1842-1879: Gandji Sindje Adjahoutonon

1879-1894: Gigla Nodon Gbenon Maou Adjahoutonon

1894: February the 4th, France removes Allada from under the kingdom of Danxomè

1894-1898: Gigla Gounhou Hougnon Adjahoutonon

1898-1909: Djihento Adjahoutonon

1909: France completes its annexation of Allada and significantly reduces the powers of its King.

1909-1923: Chief Djihento

1923-1954: Chief Kanfon

1954-19XX: Chief Gigla

1960: Dahomey becomes independent.

1992-present: King Kpodegbe Djigla

Rulers Mahi of the Kingdom of Savalou

Founding of the kingdom of Savalou around 1600

Gbaguidi I Soha Agba Rhako (1600-1618)

Adigli (regent) (1618-1657)

Betete Ava (regent) (1657-1700)

Gnahoui Kpoki (regent) (1700-1722)

Gbaguidi II Tchaou Aditi (1722-1769)

Gbaguidi III Baglo (1769-1794) (installé par Kpengla)

Gbaguidi IV Djeyizo Bonanaglo (1794-1804)

Gbaguidi V Badébou (1804-1818)

Gbaguidi VI Gougnisso (1818-1860)

Gbaguidi VII Lintonon (1860-1878)

Gbaguidi VIII Zoundégla (1878-1901) (Zoundegla Nozin Wandodo) (signed a protectorate with France represented by General Amédée Dodds)

Gbaguidi IX Goumoan (1901-1928)

Gbaguidi X Bahinnou (1928-1937)

Gbaguidi XI Gandigbé (1937-1983)

Gbaguidi XII Houessolin (1983-2002)

Throne is vacant (2002-2006)

Gbaguidi XIII Tossoh (2006-2014)

Gbaguidi XIV Gandjegni Awoyo (2014-present)

Kings of Hogbonou (Porto-Novo)

Phase 1: Kingdom of the Agassouvi Allada-Tadonous
1688-1729: TE AGBANLIN, King fondateur
1729-1739: Hiakpon, King
1739-1746: Lokpon, King
1746-1752: Houde, King
1752-1757: Messi (I), King
1757-1761: Houyi, King
1761-1765: Gbeyon, King
1765-1775: Throne is vacant
1775-1783: Ayikpe, King
1783-1794: Ayaton, King

Phase 2: Adjatche Kingdom
1794-1807: HOUFFON, King
1807-1816: Ajohan, King
1816-1818: Toyi Tofa (I), King
1818-1828: Houeze, King
1828-1836: Toyon, King
1836-1848: Meyi, King
1848-1864: Sodji, King
1864-1872: Mikpon, King
1872-1874: Messi (II), King
1874-1908: TOFA (II), King (most known)

Phase 3: Kingdom after French annexation in 1908

1908-1913: Gbedessin Tofa (III), chief

1913-1929: Houdji, chief

1929-1930: Toli, chief

1930-1941: Gbehinto, chief

1941-194X: Gbesso Toyi, chief

194X-1976: ALOHINTO GBEFFA, chief

Rulers of the Bariba Kingdom of Parakou
(born from the Nikki Kingdom around year 1700)

Kobourou Akpaki Duro Bekuru I
Akpaki Atagara
Akpaki Timkpopo
Akpaki Yereku
Akpaki Gobinyesse
Akpaki Tinra I
Akpaki Buku Kene I
Buru Borassi
Akpaki Lafia I (18XX-1894)
Buru Gingirekpunon (1894-1895)
Buru Donborigi (1895-1895)
Buru Gessere (1895-1927)
Akpaki Tinra II (1927-1942)
Buru Donkakuson (1942-1952)
Akpaki Duro Bekuru II (1952-1974)
Akpaki Lafia II (1974-1995)
Akpaki Dagbara (1995-2004)
Tchabi Mama (2004-2012)
Akpaki Buku Kene II (2012-present)

Rulers of the Berba Kingdom of Kouandé (Gwandé)

Kasa
Wimbo Kasa I
Kandikoni
Nyami I
Dari
Kunyati
Sakwa
Ikori
Wimbo Kasa II
Nambo
Nyami II
Yani

Rulers of the Bariba Borgou Kingdom of Nikki (Sarkin Nikki)

Kingdom founded by Sunon Sero

Sime Doboudya
Kpe Gunu Giribussike
Sero Kpera I Illorikpunon
Sina Boagi Ningurumekpunon
Kpe Gunu I Yoromkire Bio Bukari
Sero Kpera II Niamarekpunon (18XX-1837)
Sero Kpe Lafia I (1837-18XX)
Sero Kora I
Kpe Sumera Karakoari Toboku
Sero Tasu I
Sero Toru Munko Sina Turinka (18XX-1897)
Kpe Sumera (1898-1901)
Sina Toru Passo Suanru (1901-1915)
Kisra Pruka (1915-1917)
Sero Naina (1917-1924)
Kisra Yeruma Seru Toru Tanku (1924-1928)
Sero Kpera III (1928-1932)
Kpe Gunu II Kora Gari (1932-1938)
Kpe Gunu III Tchabi Yerima (1938-1952)
Kpe Lafia II (1952-1957)
Sero Kpera IV Saka Mivera (1957-1970)
Sero Tasu II Isakpe Gunu (1970-1991)
Sero Kora II Yerima Banesi (1991-present)

Rulers of the Bariba Borgou Kingdom of Kouandé

1790: Founding of the kingdom by Worou Wari, son of Chabi Gaba who fled from Nikki.

Worou Wari I Taboufoura (1790-1804)

Worou Sourou I Baba Tantame (1804-1816)

Sorou I (1816-1833)

Bio Doko (1833-1833)

Boukou Ya Dari Ginimou Sikou (1833-1852)

Wonkourou Tabouko (1852-1883)

Worou Wari II (1883-1897)

Souanrou (1898-1904)

Gounou Deke (1904-1929)

Worou Sourou II (1929-1943)

Sorou II (1943-1949)

Worou Wari III Tounkou Cessi (1950-1957)

Imorou Dogo (1958-1961)

                                        (1961-1996) Throne is vacant

Worou Sourou II (1996-2005)

Sorou III (2005-present)

All Kings of Kouande carry the title of "Banga" which means "Bull"

Rulers of the Ewé Kingdom of Agoué

1812: Founding of the kingdom

Komlagan (1812-1821), son of Quam Dessou

Akouete Lawson Katraya (1821-1833)

Agounou (1833-1834)

Toji (1834-1844)

Kponton I Avoumbe (1844-1846)

Hanto Tona (1846-1858)

Soji Komin Agidi (1858-1873)

Atanle (1873-1889)

Ahlonko Boutiyi (1889-1894)

Kouassihela Diogo (1894-1895)

1895: Kingdom annexed by France

Throne is vacant (1895-1901)

1901: Kingdom resumes under French/German colonial control

Abalo Bajavi (1901-1930)

Kofi Titriwe (1930-1935)

Throne is vacant (1935-1937)

Augustino Olympio (1937-1945)

Throne is vacant (1945-1946)

Kponton II (1946-1949)

Rulers of the Bariba and Borgou Kingdom of Kandi

Founding of the kingdom around 1700

Saka Bagu I
Saka Bukunene
Saka Barikali II
Saka Minti II
Saka Kina Dogo Donsarukpunon
Saka Gezere II
Saka Lafia II (19XX-1911)
Saka Zibiri II (1911-1929)
Saka Bagu II (1929-19XX)
Saka Sabi Goro (19XX-19XX)

Saka = King

Rulers of the Gourmantche Kingdom of Djougou

Founding of the kingdom around 1700

Gourma Dynasty
1800-1815 Banga Nyora II
1815-18XX Kpe Toni II
18XX-18XX Kurugu IV Atakora
18XX-1880 Nyora III
1880-1899 Kpe Toni III
1899-1900 Baba Jimba
1900-19XX Atakora
19XX-19XX Kpe Toni IV
19XX-19XX Kpe Toni V
19XX-19XX Kpe Toni VI

Rulers of the Yoruba Kingdom of Kétou

Around 1500, the Yoruba kingdom moved its capital to Kétou. In 1886, Kétou was fully annexed by the Kingdom of Danxomè. In 1893, the Kingdom of Kétou is reinstated but under a French protectorate. To this date Kétou had have 51 Kings.

Number	Name	Parents of the King	Family	Ruling Years and Comments
Kings in Aro (Nigeria) before the migration to Dahomey				
1	Şopasan (Shopashan)	Paluku & Olu-wunku (both born in Ile-Ife)	Aro	He led the migration from Ile-Ife to Aro
2	Owe	Adeyomu & Asebi	Aro	
3	Ajoje	Ademunle & Odere	Aro	
4	Itcha (Ija) Ikpachan	(Unkown dad) & Ofinran	Aro	
5	Erankikan	Adebiyi & Oju	Aro	
6	Agbo-Akoko (Agbo I) AlaKétou	Adekambi & Oliji (princess and daughter of King Oduduwa of Ile-Ife)	Aro	
Kings in Kétou (Benin/Dahomey)				
7	Ede	Unknown Parents	Aro	Around year 1500, King Ede led the migration from Aro to Kétou. He later gave the name Alaloumon to one of his sons in honor of the hunter who pointed them to where to settle, around a big tree (Kétou)
8	Okoyi	Atonsi & Oniyi		
9	Esu	Aro-bada-Isa & Agba		
10	Apanhum	Adunu & Awopa		
11	Daro	Anepo & Orere		
12	Ogo	Adimu & Asanu	Alapini	
13	Agbo-keji (Agbo II)	Ajido & Oduola		
14	Sa	Aguro & Asabi		Built the city walls and the magic doors of Kétou
15	Epo	Lilaja & Iroku		
16	Ajina	Asubo & Abesu		
17	Ara	Akambi & Ofere		
18	Odiyi Koyenikan	Parents inconnus		
19	Olukadun	Adekambi & Ajaro		
20	Arugbo	Ajagbe & Ijaku		

21	Odun	Atişe & Ajọke		
22	Tete	Ajido & Adufẹ		
23	Ajiboyede	Iroro & Awele		
24	Arowojoye	Akoni & Kobolu		
25	Epo Otudi	Omowoye & Ajini	Mesa	
26	Etu	Ondofoyi & Awopẹ	Mefu	
27	Ekoshoni	Agbaka & Abero	Alapini	
28	Emuwagun	Adisa & Aşakẹ	Magbo	
29	Asunu	Aşotan & Iyamo	Aro	
30	Agodogbo	Ileju & Asabo	Mesa	
31	Agasu	Ajagbe & Ayinke	Mefu	
32	Orubu	Aşuloye & Agbekẹ	Alapini	
33	Ileke	Adike & Koraye	Magbo	
34	Ebo	Adiro & Anikẹ	Aro	
35	Osuyi	Akande & Aşakẹ	Mesa	
36	Oniyi	Ojugbele & Abẹşe	Mefu	
37	Abiri	Aşotan & Awẹle	Alapini	
38	Oje	(Unknown dad) & Ilufẹ	inconnu	1748 - 1760
39	Ande	Adeyi & (Mère inconnue)	Magbo	1760 - 1780
40	Akebioru	Ibajẹ & (Mère inconnue)	Aro	1780 - 1795
41	Ajibolu	Orubu & Aşabi	Mesa	1795 - 1816
42	Adebiya	Orubu & Adubo	Mefu	1816 - 1853
43	Adegbede	Asunu & Owuaji	Alapini	1853 – 1858 loyal friend to King Guézo of Danxome, he killed himself in despair when Guézo was killed with an arrow on his way to seeking refuge in his palace during a military campaign
44	Adiro	Obaleke & Obasi	Magbo	1858 - 1867
45	Osun Ojẹku	(Unknown dad) & Wenfolu	Aro	1867 – 1883 was beheaded by the army of King Glèlè when he was avenging the death of his father Guézo
Regent	Agidigbo Hungbo			1883-1886 Regent appointed by King Glèlè to rule over Kétou

Throne is vacant (1886-1893) after full destruction of the kingdom by Glèlè

Regent	Ida				1893-1894 The kingdom is taken by France from Danxome, reinstated under a French Protectorate, and a regent is appointed.
46	Oyingin	Abido & Oluwofe		Mesa	1894 – 1918 The kingdom of Kétou is born again.
47	Ademufękun Dudu	Odewena & Ilemole		Mefu	1918 - 1936
48	Adegbitę Alamu Adewori	Ogun & Alaye		Alapini	1937 - 1963
49	Adetutu			Magbo	1965 - 2002
Throne is vacant (2002-2005)					
50	Aladé Ifè (b.1948 Basile Gbotche)			Aro	2005 - 2018
51	Adedun Loyé Akanni Aderomola (b. Anicet Adédjouman Adéchinan)			Mesa	2018 – present

One parameter that adds a lot of complexity to the genealogy of the kings of Kétou is the fact that the throne is not directly passed from the king to one of his children. The process is a lot different. Since the kings started using the title of Alaketou, the throne rotates between five royal families: Alapini, Aro, Mecha (Mesa), Magbo and Mefou.

The Presidents of Dahomey (Benin)

Hubert Maga (1916-2000) *1960-1963*

1963 Military Coup

Christophe Soglo (1912-1984) *1963-1964*

1964 Elections

Sourou Migan Apithy (1913-1989) *1964-1965*

Two 1965 Military Coups

Tahirou Congakou (1911-1993) **Nov - Déc 1965**

Christophe Soglo (1912-1984) *1965-1967*

1967 Military Coup

Maurice Kouandete (1932-2003) *1 jour en 1967*

Alphonse Alley (1930-x) *1967-1968*

Emile Derlin Zinsou (1918-2016) *1968-1969*

1969 Military Coup

Maurice Kouandete (1932-2003) *3 jours en 1969*

Paul Emile de Souza (1931-1999) *1969-1970*

Hubert Maga (1916-2000) *1970-1972*

Justin T. Ahonmandegbe (1917-2002) **Mai-Oct 1972**

1972 Military Coup

Mathieu Kerekou (1933-2015) *1972-1991*

1991 Elections

Nicephore Soglo (1934-x) *1991-1996*

1996 and 2001 Elections

Mathieu Kerekou (1933-2015) *1996-2006*

2006 and 2011 Elections

Thomas Boni Yayi (1952-x) *2006-2016*

2016 Elections

Patrice Talon (1958-x) *2016-present*

European Rulers in Dahomey/Benin

Portuguese Governors (1680-1961) of Ouidah in Dahomey

1680-17xx Jacinto de Figueiredo e Abreu (builder of the Fort)

17xx-1721 *Vacant*

1721-1732 Francisco Pereira Mendes

1732-1736 Manuel Correia da Cunha

1736-1743 João Basílio

1743-1746 Martinho de Cunha Barbosa

1746-1746 Francisco Nunes Pereira (usurper)

1746-1746 Francisco do Espírito Santo

1746-1752 Filipe José de Gouveia

1752-1759 Teodósio Rodrigues da Costa

1759-1760 António Nunes de Gouveia

1760-1790 Félix José de Gouveia

1790-1797 Francisco António da Fonseca e Aragão

1797-1817 Manuel Bastos Varela Pinto Pacheco

1817-1844 Francisco Félix de Sousa (Chacha)

1844-1845 Joaquim José Libânio

1845-1848 Francisco Félix de Sousa (Chacha)

1849-1851 Quaresma

1851-1851 Alferes Elerpech

1851-1852 Isidoro Félix de Sousa

1852-1853 João Justino da Costa

1853-1858 José Pinheiro de Sousa

1858-1858 Francisco Félix de Sousa (Chacha)

1858-1865 *Vacant*

1865-1868 José Maria Borges de Sequeira
1868-1869 *Vacant*
1869-1872 Vital de Bettencourt de Vasconcellos
1872-187x António Joaquim
187x-1878 Augusto Frutuoso de Figueiredo de Barros
1878-1879 Lourenço da Rocha
1879-1881 António José Machado
1881-1883 *Unknown*
1883-1885 Fernando Gonçalves
1885-1885 Bernardo Francisco Luís da Cruz
1885-1885 José Gomes de Sousa
1885-1886 Francisco Rego
1886-1887 António Domingues Cortez da Silva Curado
1887-1888 Manuel Francisco Rodrigues Guimarães
1888-1888 Vicente da Rosa Rolim
1888-1890 Manuel José Ferreira dos Santos
1890-1890 Carolino Acácio Cordeiro
1890-1893 Vicente da Rosa Rolim
1893-1897 Manuel José Ferreira dos Santos
1897-1898 Lieutenant Campos
1898-1900 Nunes de Aguiar
1900-190x António Mendes da Costa
190x-1905 João de Deus Pires
1905-1906 Joaquim Luís de Carvalho
1906-1909 *Unknown*
1909-1911 Sebastião Lousada
1911-1911 Cândido João de Barros
1911-1912 Guilherme Spínola de Melo

1912-191x *Unknown*

191x-1928 Viriato Henrique dos Anjos Garcez

1928-1931 Joaquim Sinel de Cordes

1931-1932 *Vacant*

1932-1938 Miguel Maria Pupo Correia

1938-1941 José Pimenta Segurado de Avelar Machado

1941-1942 Jean-Louis Bourjac (self-proclaimed)

1942-1944 José de Vasconcelos e Sá Guerreiro Nuno

1944-1946 Carlos Alberto de Serpa Soares

1946-1946 José de Vasconcelos e Sá Guerreiro Nuno

1946-1951 Miguel Maria Pupo Correia

1951-1954 António João Teles Pereira de Vasconcelos

1954-1956 Ernesto António Pereira Enes

1956-1961 António Agostinho Saraiva Borges

This list is invaluable because it sheds some light on the origins of multiple beninese families with Portuguese names and roots. Some of those governors dated and impregnated some local beninese women and their offspring continue to this day to enrich the beninese sociocultural landscape. Some of the family names remained the same; others were modified through time. Most of the families live in Ouidah, Cotonou and other coastal cities.

French Governors (1900-1960) of Porto-Novo in Dahomey

1894-1900	Victor Ballot
1900-1902	Victor Liotard
1902-1902	Charles Marchal
1903-1903	Eugène Decazes
1904-1904	Julien Penel
1904-1906	Victor Liotard
1906-1908	Charles Marchal
1908-1908	Edmond Gaudart
1908-1909	Jean Peuvergne
1909-1909	Raphaël Antonetti
1909-1910	Henri Malan
1911-1911	Raphaël Antonetti
1911-1912	Émile Merwart
1912-1917	Charles Noufflard
1917-1928	Gaston Fourn
1928-1928	Lucien Geay
1928-1930	Dieudonné Reste
1931-1932	Théophile Tellier
1932-1933	Louis Aujas
1933-1933	Louis Blacher
1933-1934	Marcel de Coppet
1934-1934	Camille Théodore Raoul Maillet
1934-1934	Marcel Alix Jean Marchessou

1934-1935	Jean Desanti
1935-1937	Maurice Bourgine
1937-1937	Henri Martinet
1937-1937	Louis Alexis Étienne Bonvin
1937-1939	Ernest Gayon
1938-1941	Armand Annet
1941-1944	Léon Truitard
1944-1945	Charles André Assier de Pompignan
1945-1946	Marc Laurent de Villedeuil
1946-1948	Robert Legendre
1948-1948	Jean Chambon
1948-1951	Jacques Boissier
1949-1951	Claude Valluy
1951-1955	Charles-Henri Bonfils
1955-1958	Casimir Marc Biros
1958-1960	René Tirant

Political Phases of the Dahomey/Benin History

- Various settlements and migratory movements: From the Origins to the 12th century.
- Old Kingdom of Allada, Kingdom of Danxomè and Other Kingdoms: 12th century-1900
- French Colony: 1900-1960
- Republic of Dahomey: 1960-1975
- People's Republic of Benin: 1975-1990
- Republic of Benin: 1990-present

Political Phases of the French Empire

Carolingian Empire 751-843

Split of Verdun August 11th in the year of 843

First French Colonial Empire 843-1815

Treaty of Versailles 1783

Fall of Napoleon and return to royalty: June 22, 1815

Second French Colonial Empire 1815-1946

French Union 1946-1958

French Community 1958-1960

Francafrique and Francophonie 1960-present

Phases of French presence in Benin

First contacts: 17th century (1600s).

First French Fort in West Africa (St Louis in Senegal) in 1659.

Trade and exchanges between Africans and Caucasians as equal partners between1659 and 1886.

1861: England bombarded Porto-Novo

1863: Porto-Novo agreed to a French Protectorate.

1884-1885: Berlin Conference to draw the borders of European colonies in Africa, and therefore of future African countries in the absence of the main stakeholders. This was during the reign of King Glèlè of Danxomè.

1886: France decides unilaterally to add Benin to its empire (The 2nd French Empire)

1890: King Behanzin disagrees and war starts with France.

1st France-Dahomey War (21 Feb 1890 - 4 Oct 1890): Dahomey loses. France takes Cotonou on top of Porto-Novo and Kinto.

2nd France-Dahomey War (4 Jul 1892 - 15 Jan 1894): Dahomey loses. France totally takes over Dahomey with an official decree on June 22, 1894.

Autonomous colony of Dahomey 1894-1904

French West Africa 1904-1946

French Union 1946-1958

French community 1958-1960

CFA franc zone and Francophonie 1960-present

List of Photos and Illustrations

- Map of migrations by Yoruba, Fon, and Ewe people, D.T. Niane
- Map of Dahomey, 1892, Le Petit Journal
- Emblems of the Rulers of Danxomè
- Contemporary map of Bénin
- Surrender of Gbèhanzin to général Amédée Dodds
- The Danxomè army going to war, 1793, Archibald Dalzel
- Illustration of King Guézo 1
- Illustration of King Guézo 2
- Illustration of a French attack foiled by the Danxomè army, 1892, Le Petit Journal
- Illustration of the annual feasts and customs in Danxomè, 1793, Archibald Dalzel
- Illustration of the army of Gbèhanzin, 1902, L'intransigeant
- Mural of King Guézo
- Photo of Kpalin-gan, Bas relief, 1972, Spini et Antogini
- Photo of Bas relief depicting the first encounter with europeans, 1994, Francesca Pique
- Photo of one of the thrones of King Guézo
- Photo of Bas relief depicting a fight between a Fon soldier and a Yoruba soldier, 1986, Suzanne Preston Blier
- Photo of King Agonglo's Assin, Jean Pliya
- Photo of Bas relief depicting the planting of the flag of Danxomè on conquered land, 1994, Susan Middleton
- Photo of King Glèlè's Adjalala, 1986, Suzanne Preston Blier
- Photo of King Guézo's Adjalala, 1926, Waterlot
- Photo of King Agoli Agbo at an old age
- Photo of young King Agoli Agbo, 1894, Getty

- Photo of amazones during the coronation of Agoli Agbo, 1894, French military doctor
- Photo of Gbèhanzin and his relatives in Algéria, 1905
- Photo of Gbèhanzin and his relatives in Martinique, 1895
- Photo of a détail of King Guézo's Adjalala, 1900
- Photo of a cannon used by Gbèhanzin
- Photo of a statue of Gbèhanzin, Goho, 2019, Fondation Medali
- Photo of King Glèlè
- Summary of the genealogy of the Kings of Danxomè, 2019, Dallys-Tom Medali

Bibliography

- 1000 African Heroes, Dallys-Tom Medali, 2017
- Archives des missions africaines à Lyon, John Duncan, 1847
- Behanzin Correspondances et Discours, Cahier de la Fondation Zinsou, 2006
- Chants et panegyrics de la reine Zognidi, Document Audio, Club Hanye Ounkpeou, 2017
- Dahomey, an ancient West-African kingdom, Melville J. Herskovits, 1938
- De l'igname au manioc dans le golfe de Guinée, Dominique Juhé-Beaulaton, 2014
- Histoire des populations Mahi, Sylvain Anignikin, Cahiers d'études africaines, vol. 162, 2001
- Histoire du Benin - CM1, Firmin Medenouvo,
- Histoire de mon pays, Jean Pliya, 1971
- Histoire Générale de l'Afrique, UNESCO, Auteurs Multiples, Livres I, II, III, IV, V
- L'historique de la Collectivité Ade Kplankoun de Houawe Koulogon, Ade Koulo Lambert, 2015
- La pensée symbolique des Fons du Dahomey, thèse de Claude Savary, Genève, 1976
- La succession au trône de Houegbadja perpétuée au sein de la lignée Agoli Agbo, ADARA, 2008
- Le Dahomey, Gouvernement General de l'Afrique Occidentale Française, 1906
- Les Fon et les Yoruba, du Delta du Niger au Cameroun, E. J. Alagoa, Livre V
- The first Chacha of Whydah, David Ross, 1969
- The Abomey Royal Palaces, Getty

- The History of the Yorubas: From the earliest times to the beginning of the British Protectorate, Samuel Johnson, 1921
- The impact of European Settlement within French West Africa, Elise Huillery, 2009
- Origines de Savalou et ses Kings, Paris, Émile Larose, coll. « Littérature de l'Afrique noire », 1928
- Récits de voyage du britannique Robert Norris au XVIIIe siècle, 1955
- Rois, Princes, Nobles et Esclaves, Dallys-Tom Medali, 2019
- Tradition Orale - Divers Interviews
- Une Reine, Trois rois, Un Destin - Critiques et récits historiques de la vie de Djeto Francisca Zognidi, Toussaint C. Ahomagnon, 2017
- Wanderings in West Africa, Richard F. Burton, 1863
- Wikipedia - Divers Articles
- Wives of the Leopard: Gender, Politics, and Culture in the Kingdom of Dahomey, Edna Bay, 1998

Other Books by the same Author

1. Légendes Inédites d'Afrique (fairy tales)
2. 1000 African Heroes (non-fiction)
3. 1000 Héros Africains (non-fiction)
4. Le Manuel du Milliardaire (non-fiction)
5. 10 Règles du Succès (non-fiction)
6. Essais sur le Bénin (non-fiction)
7. Poisonous Snakes in the Republic of Benin (non-fiction)
8. Red Blue and Green (art book)
9. Black and White (art book)
10. Nude and Alive (art book)
11. 30 years of Painting and Drawing (art book)
12. Perles et Pensées (poetry)
13. Coming Back (poetry)
14. Belles Poésies de Cœur et de Corps (poetry)
15. L'Evangile Pratique (religious)
16. La Bible Essentielle (religious)

Other Books in "The House of Dallys" Series

Livre 1: Les Familles de la Maison de Dallys: Kings, princes, esclaves et nobles

Livre 2: Histoire et Généalogie de la Collectivité Medali

Livre 3: Histoire et Généalogie de la Collectivité Tokpo

Livre 4: Histoire et Généalogie de la Collectivité Sèglé Houegbadja du Bénin

Livre 5: Histoire et Généalogie de la Collectivité Adè Koulo

Livre 6: Nan Zognidi Kpodjito, Biographie et Généalogie d'une Reine du Dahomey, Epouse de Guézo, Mère de Glèlè et Grand-mère de Béhanzin

Livre 7: Adè Kplankoun, Biographie et Généalogie du patriarche des collectivités Adè, Koulo et Autres de Houawé au Dahomey

Livre 8: Histoire et Généalogie de la Collectivité Agassounon du Bénin

Livre 9: Tables généalogiques de Yulia Sassina et de Philibert Dimigou en Russie et au Bénin

Livre 10: Généalogie et Histoire des Kings du Dahomey (Tome 1 et Tome 2)

Livre 11: Etudes Généalogiques sur diverses familles du Sud Bénin (not yet published)

Livre 12: Origine des Peuples Fons d'Afrique (not yet published)

Contacts

If you have any information, archives, documents, or suggestions to share with us, or if you want to order more copies,

Please reach out by mail to:

PO-BOX 04-0143, Cotonou, Republic of Benin
or
5829 N 29th St Omaha, NE 68111, USA
or
email: dallys@livres.us

www.dallystom.com
www.heroafricain.com
www.livres.us

ISBN 978-1-947838-38-3

www.ingramcontent.com/pod-product-compliance
Lightning Source LLC
Chambersburg PA
CBHW030817190426
43197CB00036B/561